Henry H. Woodbury

Complete History of the 46th Illinois Veteran Volunteer Infantry

Henry H. Woodbury

Complete History of the 46th Illinois Veteran Volunteer Infantry

ISBN/EAN: 9783337399221

Printed in Europe, USA, Canada, Australia, Japan

Cover: Foto ©ninafisch / pixelio.de

More available books at **www.hansebooks.com**

COMPLETE HISTORY

OF THE

46TH ILLINOIS VETERAN

VOLUNTEER INFANTRY,

From the date of its organization in 1861, to its final discharge, February 1st, 1866, containing a full and authentic account of the participation of the regiment in the

Battles, Sieges, Skirmishes and Expeditions

In which it has been engaged, together with a

COMPLETE ROSTER OF THE REGIMENT,

SHOWING THE PROMOTIONS,

COMMISSIONED AND NON-COMMISSIONED,

DEATHS, DISCHARGES AND DESERTIONS.

FREEPORT, ILLINOIS.
BAILEY & ANKENY, PRINTERS.
::::::::
1866.

FIELD AND STAFF.

COLONELS.

John A. Davis, died October 10, 1862, at Bolivar, Tenn., of wounds received at battle Matamora, October 5th, 1862.
†Benjamin Dornblaser, appointed Brev. Brig. Gen'l Feb. 20, 1865.

LIEUTENANT COLONELS.

Wm. O. Jones, resigned December 31st, 1861.
†John J. Jones, appointed Brev. Colonel, June 19, 1865.

MAJORS.

Benjamin Dornblaser, appointed Colonel October 11, 1862.
John M. McCracken, mustered out December, 1864, expiration term of service.
†Joseph Clingman.

ADJUTANTS.

Benjamin Dornblaser, appointed Major February 8, 1862.
Edward R. Lord, resigned November 19, 1862.
†Henry H. Woodbury.

QUARTERMASTERS.

James L. Wilson, resigned January 15, 1862.
David S. Pride, appointed Capt. Co. I, November 24, 1862.
Edwin R. Gillett, resigned October 5, 1864.
†James B. Wright.

SURGEONS.

Elias C. DePuy, resigned September 3, 1862.
Elias C. DePuy, resigned November 1, 1864.
†Benjamin H. Bradshaw.

ASSISTANT SURGEONS.

Charles Carle, discharged April 8, 1862, to enable him to accept promotion in the 41st Ill. Infantry.
Benjamin H. Bradshaw, appointed Surgeon December 18, 1864.
†Julius N. DeWitt.

CHAPLAINS.

David Teed, resigned September 1, 1862.
Hezekiah R. Lewis, mustered out January 12, 1866.

NON-COMMISSIONED STAFF.

SERGEANT MAJORS.

Wm. Swansey, discharged for disability May 29, 1862.
Henry A. Ewing, discharged to accept promotion in colored organization, October 25, 1863.
John E. Hershey, discharged for disability September 1, 1864.
†Edgar Butterfield.

Q. M. SERGEANTS.

James Duncan, discharged for disability May 29, 1862.
James H. Davis, reduced to ranks and assigned to Company I, March 1, 1864.
James B. Wright, appointed Quartermaster November 16, 1864.
†Julius T. Weld.

COMMISSARY SERGEANTS.

Edwin R. Gillett, appointed 1st Lieutenant and R. Q. M., December 26, 1862.
‡Wm. H. Barnds.

HOSPITAL STEWARDS.

Joseph Chambers, discharged for disability, 1862.
James Steele, discharged to accept promotion in colored organization, March 1, 1864.
Thomas Woolcott, reduced to ranks and assigned to Company K, May 31, 1864.
†Thomas J. Allen.

PRINCIPAL MUSICIANS.

George A. Black, discharged for disability, May 25, 1862.
†George W. Trotter.
†Thomas W. Slade.

COMPANY "A."

CAPTAINS.

John Musser, died April 23d, 1862, of wounds received at Shiloh.
Joseph Clingman, promoted Major March 20, 1865.
†Isaac A. Arnold.

1st LIEUTENANTS.

William O. Saxton, resigned April 1st, 1862.
Isaac A. Arnold, promoted Captain March 20, 1865.
†Wm. Reynolds.

2d LIEUTENANTS.

Isaac A. Arnold, promoted 1st Lieutenant July 10, 1862.
George S. Dickey, resigned November 9, 1864.
William Reynolds, promoted 1st Lieutenant March 20, 1865.
†William R. Moore.

1st SERGEANTS.

Joseph Clingman, promoted Captain June 26, 1862.
Quincy E. Pollock, died April 9, 1862, of wounds received at Shiloh.
Adam Kemper, discharged November 14, 1863, to receive promotion in 6th U. S. C. Art.
John W. Taylor, reduced to ranks May 1st, 1864.
Wm. R. Moore, promoted 2d Lieutenant March 20, 1865.
†Shepard A. French.

SERGEANTS.

George S. Dickey, promoted 2d Lieutenant July 20, 1862.
Horace D. Purinton, discharged December 12, 1863, to receive promotion in colored organization.
Wm. Reynolds, promoted to 2d Lieutenant March 3d, 1865.
Shepard A. French, appointed 1st Sergeant April 1st, 1865.
John Hart, mustered out June 19, 1865— War Department order.
†John Sheckler.
†Robert P. Ritzman.
†James Van Brocklin.
Oscar B. Fowler, reduced to ranks February 1st, 1862.
Daniel A. Galpin   "   "   October 1st, 1862.
Benjamin Musser, discharged November 24, 1862.
†James H. Mack.

CORPORALS.

Andrew M. Fellows, died May 2d, 1862, of wounds received at Shiloh.
Wesley J. Best, reduced to ranks.
James H. Mack, appointed Sergeant August 1st, 1865.
†George W. Bolender.
Daniel M. Hart, discharged July 8th, 1862.
James M. Van Brocklin, appointed Sergeant April 1st, 1865.
Robert P. Ritzman, appointed Sergeant March 3d, 1865.
†Charles Clingman.
Thomas S. Clingman, discharged August 2d, 1862.
†Daniel A. Scoville.
Albert M. Lull, discharged October 2d, 1862.
John Sheckler, appointed Sergeant January 1st, 1864.
†Robert P. Wilson.
Aml F. Arnold, killed at battle Shiloh, April 6th, 1862.
Adam Kemper, appointed 1st Sergeant October 1st, 1862.
James Reim, died of disease March 22, 1864.
†Robert Patten.
Benj. Musser, appointed Sergeant October 1st, 1862.
†Wm. F. Early.

Robert D. Brunner, died of disease October 6th, 1864.
†Hilliary Buss.
Quincy E. Pollock, appointed 1st Sergeant March 1st, 1862.
Harrison W. Bolender, discharged August 25, 1862.
Daniel R. Rubendall, mustered out June 10, 1865.
†Thomas W. Evans.
James M. Babcock, discharged November 25, 1863, to receive promotion in colored organization.

PRIVATES.

Arnold Ami F., appointed Corporal Sept. 10, 1861.
Arnold Albert E., discharged Sept. 4, 1862.
Andre Wm., vet., died of disease Dec. 10, 1864.
Allison Wm. W., died of disease March 10, 1863.
†Andre Jacob D., vet., transferred from B Co. April 1, 1864.
†Ambrose DeWitt, C.
†Allen John A., transferred from 99th Illinois Infantry.
†Askeu John A., transferred from 99th " "
Barnds Wm. H., vet., appointed Comissary Sergeant, transferred to non-commissioned Staff, Jan. 1, 1864.
Bates Andrew J., discharged July 9, 1862.
Barrett Charles, discharged Aug. 13, 1862.
Best Wesley J., vet., appointed Corporal Oct. 1, 1864—died Aug. 14, 1864, of wounds received at battle Jackson, Miss.
Benton Martin, discharged Nov. 24, 1862.
Best Robt. F., died Nov. 2, 1861, of disease.
Buss Hilliary, vet., appointed Corporal Aug. 1, 1865.
Bolender Harrison W. appointed Corporal March 1, 1862,
Bolender Geo. W., vet., appointed Corporal Jan. 1, 1864.
Babcock James M. appointed Corporal Dec. 1, 1862.
Barrett Edward, died of disease, Aug. 12, 1864.
Bruner Robt. D., appointed Corporal May 30, 1864.
Brown Charles, discharged May 8, 1865.
Best Hiram C., discharged June 19, 1865.
†Belknap Corwin.
Ceam William, transferred to Veteran Reserve Corps, Aug. 4, 1863.
†Clingman Abner, veteran.
†Clingman George R., veteran.
Clingman Thomas S., appointed Corporal Sept. 10, 1861.
Clingman Charles, vet., appointed Corporal Jan. 1, 1864.
Clingman Joseph, appointed 1st Sergeant Sept. 10, 1861.
Clause Charles, died of disease, Sept. 7, 1862.
Carter Sherwood E., vet., transferred to Co. I, Nov. 1, 1864.
†Clause Thilman.
†Clingman John T.
†Clingman William.
†Cadwell Horace.
†Clow Benjamin.
Cousins Albert, transferred from 99th Ills. Infantry—mustered out term expired Oct., 1865.
Derrick James E., discharged May 28, 1862.
DeHaven Daniel P., died of disease, Sept. 22, 1862.
Dickey George S., appointed Sergeant Sept. 10, 1861.
Davidson George W., discharged April 28, 1863.
†Daughenbaugh Christian.
†Dinges John P.
Earley Wm. F., vet., appointed Corporal April 1, 1865.
Elliott John, killed in action, April 6, 1862.
Ewing Henry A., transferred to non-commissioned Staff, June 1, 1862.
Evans Thomas W., appointed Corporal Aug. 1, 1865.
†Ellis Eli.
Fellows Andrew M., appointed Corporal Sept. 10, 1861.
French Shepard A., vet., appointed Sergeant July 20, 1862.
Fowler Oscar B., appointed Sergeant Sept. 10, 1861—deserted Aug. 28, 1862.
Fauver Robert A., vet., drowned Aug. 20, 1864.
†Fauver Amos.
Fellows George E., discharged May 15, 1865.
†French David H.
French Truman A., discharged June 19, 1865.
†Ford Wm. D.
Foster Jasper, transferred from 99th Ills. Infantry—mustered out expiration of term of service, Oct., 1865.
†Garrison David W., vet.
Galpin David A. appointed Sergeant, March 1, 1862—dropped from rolls March 3, 1865.
Galpin Hiram C., discharged July 8, 1862.
†Gibbons Thomas, vet.
†Gibbons Wm., vet.
Gillett Edwin R., transferred to non-commissioned Staff, Sept. 15, 1861.
Green Christopher, deserted Aug. 21, 1862.
Gatliff Thomas C., discharged June 5, 1865.
†Glynn James.
†Gorman Lawrence G.
†Garrard Warren.

Hathaway Homer, transferred from Co. B, Nov. 1, 1862—re-enlisted in 2d. Ills. Lt. Artillery, Dec., 1863.
†Hart James H., vet.
Hart Daniel M., appointed Corporal Sept. 10, 1861.
Holsinger Wm. H., died of disease, April 1, 1862.
Hollenback Henry W., died May 3, 1862, of wounds received at Shiloh.
Hoot John, killed at Shiloh, April 6, 1862.
†Hunting Wm. A.
Hunting Chas. H., vet., discharged July 4, 1864, to receive promotion in colored organization.
Hunting Geo. H., vet., discharged Set. 18, 1864, to receive promotion in colored organization.
Hart John, appointed Sergeant Dec. 1, 1862..
†Hart Thomas J.
†Hartzell William
†Huddleston Reuben H.
Hart Joseph E.
†Hill John.
†Hills Henry M.
†Hoyman Henry.
†Hadsell Nathan A., transferred from 99th Ills.
†Hadsell Almond C.,   "   "   "   "
†Jeffries Joseph, vet.
Joy Benedict, discharged July 11, 1865.
Kemper Adam, appointed Corporal April 7, 1862..
†Krape Wm. W.
Lull Albert M., appointed Corporal Sept..10, 1861.
LeFevre Francis J., died April 9, 1862, of wounds received at Shiloh.
†Law John H.
†Lee Lorenzo H.
Luzzader George, transferred from 99th Ills. Infantry—mustered out expiration of term, Oct., 1865.
Moore Chas. F., died of disease, April 2, 1863.
Musser Benjamin, appointed Corporal Sept. 10, 1861.
Mack James H., vet., appointed Corporal Jan. 1, 1864..
Mason John H., discharged Nov. 24, 1862.
McCarty James C., vet., died of disease, March 19, 1865.
McHoes John, transferred to V. R. C., Nov. 10, 1863.
†Miller Henry W., vet.
Moore Wm. R., vet., appointed 1st Sergeant May 1, 1864.
†Musser James, vet.
May Willard F., died of disease, May 18, 1864..
†Miller Israel.
†McAffee Robt. L. H.
†Moore Geo. W.
†Moser William.
†Musser Charles.
†Moser Edwin A.
†Morgan Henry W.
†Neil Wm. R.
Patten John, killed in action, Shiloh April 6, 1862.
Parish Pleasant, transferred to B Co., Nov. 1, 1862.
Patten Robert, vet., appointed Corporal April 1, 1865.
Peck Theodore, died of disease, Jan. 8, 1862.
Peek Adelbert, discharged Nov. 29, 1864..
Pollock Quincy E. appointed Corporal Sept..10, 1861..
†Plowman Charles E., vet.
Purinton Horace D., appointed Sergeant Sept. 10, 1861.
†Parker John.
Pine George W., transferred from 99th Ills. Infantry—mustered out expiration of term, Oct., 1865.
†Quiggle Robert H., vet.
Reynolds Wm. vet., appointed Sergeant Sept. 10, 1861.
Ritzman Robert P., vet., appointed Corporal Jan. 1, 1864.
Rein James, vet., appointed Corporal Aug. 1, 1862.
Rogers David E., vet., died of disease, Dec. 12, 1864.
Rogers Henry G., killed in action at Shiloh, April 6, 1862.
Rodimer Wm. H., killed in action at Shiloh, April 6, 1862.
Rollins Eliphalet, died of disease, June 29, 1862.
Rush John, discharged Aug. 16, 1862..
†Rice Milton A.
†Reiniger Samuel J.
Rudy John, discharged May 22, 1865..
Rubendall Daniel R., appointed Corporal May 30, 1864.
†Ritzman John.
Smith Eliphalet W., transferred to V. R. C., March 26, 1864.
Scoville Daniel A., vet., appointed Corporal May 30, 1864.
Scoville Nelson, died April 18, 1862, of wounds received at Shiloh.
Sheckler John, vet., appointed Corporal Aug. 1, 1862.
†Silis Edwin, vet.
Sleight Samuel A., discharged May 3, 1863..
†Smith Church H., vet.
Smith Franklin, deserted Aug. 28, 1862.

Soloman John C., discharged May 28, 1862.
Stephens James M., died of disease, May 9, 1862.
Steele Alexander J., died of disease, July 24, 1863.
†Scoville Alfred B.
Seidel Chas. H., died of disease, Nov. 20, 1864.
†Shadel Samuel P.
†Shadle Adam C.
†Sheetz Geo. W.
†Shellenberger John.
†Smith James C.
†Swartz John L.
†Sanborn Charles G.
†Sills Thomas.
Sherman Leonard, transferred to Co. G, May 4, 1865.
Taylor John W., appointed Sergeant Dec. 1, 1863—discharged Jan. 29, 1865.
Thompson James M., died April 1, 1862, of disease.
Trotter George W., transferred to non-commissioned Staff, Jan. 1, 1864.
†Tomlins John W., transferred from B Co., April 1, 1864.
†Taft Josephus A.
Thomason Lee B., transferred from 99th Ills.—mustered out at expiration of term, Oct., 1865.
Van Brocklin James M., vet., appointed Corporal Jan. 1, 1864.
†Vinson Thomas, vet.
†Walker John W.
Werland John M., died of disease, Nov. 2, 1861.
Wisler John B., killed in action at Shiloh, April 6, 1862.
†Winchell Hiram P., vet.
Wilson Benj. F., died of disease, Dec. 30, 1861.
Wilson Robert P., vet., appointed Corporal Nov. 1, 1864.
†Windecker John, vet.
Winters Darius, discharged July 7, 1865.
†Woodring John M., discharged Nov. 24, 1862—re-enlisted Feb. 7, 1865.
†Waddell John R.
Weld Julius T., transferred to non-commissioned Staff, Jan. 18, 1865.
Wetzel Franklin T., mustered out, War Department order, June, 1865.
†Woodring Uriah, vet.
†Windecker Wm.
†Wall Thomas.
†Wright John W., transferred from 99th Ills.
†Waddell Wm. W., transferred from Co. E, Sept. 1, 1865.

COMPANY "B."

CAPTAINS.

Rollin V. Ankeny, resigned Dec. 31, 1862.
Wm. J. Reitzell, mustered out Dec. 23, 1864—expiration of term of service.
†Robert T. Cooper.

1st LIEUTENANTS.

Henry Roush, resigned April 23, 1862.
Wm. J. Reitzell, promoted Captain Feb. 28, 1863.
Emanuel Faust, resigned Oct. 5, 1864.
Robert T. Cooper, promoted Captain May 24, 1865.
Geo. S. Roush, resigned June 19, 1865.
†Thomas B. Jones.

2d LIEUTENANTS.

Thomas J. Hathaway, resigned June 10, 1862.
Wm. J. Reitzell, promoted 1st Lieut. July 16, 1862.
Emanuel Faust, promoted 1st Lieut. Feb. 28, 1863.
Robt. T. Cooper, promoted 1st Lieut. Nov. 10, 1864.
George S. Roush, promoted 1st Lieut. May 24, 1865.
Thomas B. Jones, promoted 1st Lieut. Aug. 28, 1865.
†Aaron McCauley.

1st SERGEANT.

Thomas J. Hood, promoted 1st Lieut. Co. G, Oct. 8, 1861.
Wm. J. Reitzell, promoted 2d Lieut. July 26, 1862.
Geo. S. Roush, promoted 2d Lieut. Nov. 10, 1864.
Thomas B. Jones, promoted 2d Lieut. May 14, 1865.
†John S. Hoy, vet.

SERGEANTS.

Emanuel Faust, promoted 2d Lieut. July 16, 1862.
Wm. J. Reitzell, appointed 1st Sergeant, Oct. 1, 1861.
Robert T. Cooper, promoted 2d Lieut. Feb. 28, 1863.
Robert Smith, transferred to G Co., Oct. 12, 1861.
Langford Hill, reduced to ranks at his own request, Feb. 17, 1865.
Leopold Shook, discharged July 10, 1862.

John E. Hershey, appointed Sergeant-Major Oct. 31, 1863.
Thomas B. Jones, appointed 1st Sergeant Jan. 1, 1865.
Aaron McCauley, promoted 2d Lieut. Aug. 23, 1865.
†Uriah H. Henderson, vet.
John S. Hoy, appointed 1st Sergeant Sept. 1, 1865.
†John H. Runkle, vet.
†Anson Torenzo, vet.
†Cornelius Heinnich, vet.

CORPORALS.

Geo. Cox, died Oct. 9, 1862, of wounds received at battle of Hatchie.
Leopold Shook, appointed Sergeant Oct. 2, 1861.
John E. Hershey, appointed Sergeant July 10, 1862.
Jay W. Barker, discharged Feb. 12, 1863.
John Y. Haughey, reduced to ranks at Camp Butler, Jan. 1862.
Isaac Kleckner, discharged June 14, 1862, of wounds received at Shiloh.
Geo. S. Roush, appointed 1st Sergeant March 1, 1862.
Thomas B. Jones, appointed Sergeant July 16, 1862.
Charles F. Bower, died April 23, 1862, of wounds received at Shiloh.
Aaron McCauley, appointed Sergeant March 1, 1863.
Uriah Henderson, appointed Sergeant Oct. 31, 1863.
Dayton D. Tyler, reduced to ranks Oct., 1863.
Edgar Butterfield, vet., appointed Sergeant-Major, Sept. 1, 1864.
John S. Hoy, appointed Sergeant Jan. 1, 1865.
John H. Runkle, appointed Sergeant Jan. 1, 1865.
Francis McCurdy, vet., reduced to ranks June 30, 1865—sentence of G. C. M.
†Jams From, vet.
Cornelius Heinnich, appointed Sergeant Sept. 1, 1865.
Aaron Bolender, vet., mustered out, June 19, 1865.
Norton L. Mitchell, vet., reduced to ranks Nov. 9, 1865.
†John H. Moses, vet.
Harry C. Gallaher, reduced to ranks March 24, 1865.
Alonzo W. Forbes, vet., deserted Nov. 1, 1865.
†John A. Mingle, vet.
†George McLenahen, vet.
†Adam Arnold, vet.
†Samuel Askey.
Thomas J. Shane, mustered out Sept., 1864—term expired.
Anson Turenzo, appointed Sergeant Sept. 1, 1865.
†Josiah K. Brenizer.
†Ira Erb.

PRIVATES.

Ashenfelter Cyrus, died of disease, Dec. 6, 1861.
Arnold Adam, vet., appointed Corporal Sept. 1, 1865.
†Arnold Charles, vet.
Alshause Jacob, discharged Sept. 21, 1862.
†Ansberger Sebastian, vet.
†Askey John.
Askey Samuel, promoted Corporal Sept. 1, 1865.
Artley Abraham, transferred to K Co., April 1, 1864.
†Bolender Isaac, vet.
Bolender Aaron, vet., appointed Corporal Oct. 31, 1864.
†Bolender Jackson.
†Bolender John P.
†Boyd Franklin, vet.
Barker Addison J., discharged Dec. 23, 1863.
†Barker Seymour S., vet.
†Bowen John T., vet.
Burgess Solon S., discharged June 30, 1863.
Bower Charles F., promoted to Corporal Oct. 8, 1861.
Butterfield Edgar, appointed Corporal July 1, 1862.
Blanchard David M., discharged July 13, 1862.
Barker Jay W., promoted to Corporal Sept. 10, 1861.
Broomhall John, mustered out by order, 1865.
†Braman Edwin P.
Brenizer Josiah K., appointed Corporal Nov. 9, 1865.
†Bloss Joseph L.
Crawford Franklin, mustered out, Sept. 9, 1864—term expired.
Chambers Joseph, appointed Hospital Steward, Oct. 10, 1861.
Cantrell Joel T., vet., transferred to Co. K, April 1, 1864.
Cade Charles, discharged Aug. 12, 1862.
Cooper Robert T., vet., appointed Sergeant Sept. 10, 1861.
Cox George, appointed Corporal Sept. 10, 1861.
†Carl Henry.
†Cooper Geo. W.
†Clark Silas W.
†Cooper Amos J.
†Collins Thomas, transferred from 99th Ills. Infantry.
†Colvern Geo. W., transferred from 99th Ills. Infantry.
†Chase Lewis W., transferred from 99th Ills. Infantry.
†Cochran Thomas, transferred from 99th Ills. Infantry.
Daugherty George, discharged Sept. 14, 1864.
†Dubois Wm. W.
†Daniels Willis, transferred from 99th Ills. Infantry.

†Duncan Oliver P.
†Earnst Jacob, vet.
Erb Ira, vet., appointed Corporal Nov. 9, 1865.
Ely Marion, transferred to K Co., April 1, 1864.
Forbes Alonzo W., vet., appointed Corporal April 1, 1865.
†Frankeberger Eli B., vet.
From James, vet., appointed Corporal Oct. 31, 1863.
Frieze Henry, died March 3, 1862.
Faust Emanuel, appointed Sergeant Sept. 10, 1861.
†Frankeberger Aaron.
†Fosler George.
†Gulter Adam, vet.
Gibler Hiram, mustered out Sept. 9, 1864—expiration term of service.
Gibler Joseph H., deserted July 9, 1862.
George Wm. A., died Sept. 10, 1864.
†Giddings Smith.
†Gallaher Harly C., appointed Corporal Jan. 1, 1865.
Heinnich Cornelius, vet., appointed Corporal April 1, 1864.
Hoy John S., vet., appointed Corporal July 1, 1862.
Hathaway Homer H., transferred to Co. A, Nov. 1, 1862.
†Hathaway Jeremiah J., vet.
Hathaway James B., discharged April 23, 1862.
†Hess Aaron, vet.
†Hill Langford, vet., promoted Sergeant Oct. 1, 1861.
Henderson Wm. J., vet., mustered out June 30, 1865, by War Dept. or(
†Henderson Francis M., vet.
Henderson Uriah H. vet., appointed Corporal July 1, 1862.
Hoag Charles, mustered out Sept. 9, 1864—term expired.
†Hinds Erastus, discharged Dec. 10, 1862—re-enlisted one year, Jan. 24
Hershey John E., appointed Corporal Sept. 10, 1861.
Haughey John Y., vet., appointed Corporal Sept. 10, 1861.
Hood Thomas J., appointed 1st Sergeant Sept. 10, 1861.
Hathaway Earl, transferred to G Co., Nov. 30, 1861.
Hathaway Phillip, deserted Nov. 1, 1865.
†Hine Joseph.
Hofmeister Augustus W., mustered out, Oct. 9, 1865—expiration of ter
Hendrickson Anthony, mustered out Oct. 9, 1865—expiration of term.
Hess Andrew, died April 24, 1865, of wounds received at siege of Blak(
Howe James Jr., dropped on muster out roll as a deserter.
†Hartman Henry J.
†Hartman Joseph W.
†Hamilton Thomas, transferred from 99th Ills. Infantry.
Hartzell John, mustered out Oct. 12, 1865—expiration of term.
†Inman Henry L.
Jones Thomas B., vet., appointed Corporal Sept. 10, 1861.
Johnson Wm. T., died June 17, 1865.
Kaup George, discharged July 30, 1862.
†Kryder Jacob N., vet.
Kerr Wm., mustered out Sept. 9, 1864—expiration of term.
Kellogg Eugene V., killed at Shiloh, April 7, 1862.
Kleckner Isaac, appointed Corporal Sept. 10, 1861.
King Robert, deserted March 1, 1865.
†King Edwin.
Lobdell Daniel, vet., died Oct. 3, 1865.
Long Casper, transferred to Co. G, Oct. 1, 1861.
†Lauck Jacob.
Mingle John A., vet., appointed Corporal April 1, 1865.
†Mingle David J., vet.
McCauley Aaron, vet., appointed Corporal Oct. 1, 1861.
†Mather Abijah, vet.
McElhaney Wm., discharged April 4, 1862.
McCurdy Francis, vet., appointed Corporal Oct. 6, 1863.
†Mitchell Norton L., vet., appointed Corporal Oct. 31, 1864.
Moses John H., vet., appointed Corporal Jan. 1, 1864.
McLenahan George, vet., appointed Corporal Sept. 1, 1865.
Mallory Daniel, mustered out Sept. 1, 1864—expiration of term.
Mack Harry A., died June, 1862.
Mallory John W., died May 7, 1862.
McGinnis Joseph, died Sept. 28, 1861.
†McKee Robert, vet.
†McCauley Isaac.
†Mogle Samuel.
†Mogle Jacob.
Mogle Lewis W., mustered out June, 1865—War Department order.
†McKee David.
†Mitchell Cornelius, transferred from 99th Illinois Infantry.
Nichols John, discharged Nov. 17, 1862.
Penticoff Levi, died Oct. 19, 1862.
†Pieter John, vet.
Potter Francis M., deserted July 9, 1862.
Potter Julius, died Feb. 6, 1862.
Peirce James, vet., deserted Nov. 1, 1865.
Parish Pleasant, discharged Feb. 3, 1863.

Rockwell Charles, died May 14, 1862.
Runkle John H., vet., appointed Corporal July 1, 1862.
†Runkle Wm.
Reitzell Wm. J., appointed Sergeant Sept. 10, 1861.
Roush George S., vet., appointed Corporal Sept. 10, 1861.
†Rishell Daniel L.
Roush Henry, died July 10, 1864.
†Reed Wilson D.
†Reed John P.
Stotler Jacob, died May, 1862, of wounds received at Shiloh.
Shane Charles N., died July 28, 1863.
Shane Thomas J., appointed Corporal July 1, 1862.
Shook Leopold, appointed Corporal Sept. 10, 1861.
Sprague George D., discharged Feb. 28, 1863.
Smith Robert S., appointed Sergeant Sept. 10, 1861.
†Snyder Francis M.
†Segin Theodore.
†Skinner Wm. W.
Stone Edward L., died Sept. 27, 1864.
†Seebold Calhoun.
Stanley John, mustered out, 1865—War Department order.
Shaffer Wm. F., discharged June 20, 1865.
Smith Henry, transferred from 99th Ill. Infantry—deserted Nov. 1, 1865.
Torenzo Anson, vet., appointed Corporal July 1, 1862.
Tyler Dayton D., vet., appointed Corporal July 1, 1862—transferred to D Co.
†Thompson Jonathan E.
†Thompson Robert S.
Tomlins John W., transferred to Co. A, April 1, 1864.
†Taft Henry C.
Vanmeter John C., discharged July 7, 1862.
Vinson George, vet., transferred to vet. Reserve Corps, April 25, 1865.
Vinson John, died August 12, 1864, at Morganza, La.
†Vocht Levi S.
Wilson George, died April 30, 1862.
Wright Charles F., vet., deserted Nov. 1, 1865.
Weaver David, discharged June 13, 1862.
West George, vet., discharged June 20, 1865.
Warner Wm. W., discharged July, 1862.
†Wohlford Franklin.
†Wunshel George.
†Webb Oliver P.
Wilson Henry, mustered out Oct. 9, 1865—expiration of term.
†Wagner Peter R.
Wilbur Wm. H., mustered out June, 1865—War Department order.
†Yoder Andrew B., vet.
Zeigler Miller, transferred to K Co., April 1, 1864.

COMPANY "C."

CAPTAINS.

Friedrick Krumme, resigned April 23, 1862.
Phillip Arno, mustered out December 21, 1864, expiration term of service.
†Edward Wike.

1st LIEUTENANTS.

Phillip Arno, promoted Captain April 23, 1862.
Harbert Harberts, discharged to receive promotion in 6th U. S. C. A., December 17, 1863.
Edward Wike, promoted Captain March 24, 1864.
†Andreas Olnhausen.

2d LIEUTENANTS.

Addo Borchers, resigned September 30, 1862.
Edward Wike, promoted 1st Lieutenant, April 21, 1865.
Andreas Olnhausen, promoted 1st Lieutenant March 20, 1865.
†Emil Neese.

1st SERGEANTS.

Harbert Harberts, promoted to 1st Lieutenant, April 23, 1862.
Edward Wike, promoted to 2d Lieutenant, September 30, 1862.
Robert Lang, discharged November 9, 1863, to receive promotion in 6th U. S. Artillery.
Andreas Olnhausen, promoted 2d Lieutenant, May 3, 1864.
Emil Neese, promoted to 2d Lieutenant, April 9, 1865.
Wm. Stober, reduced to Sergeant at his own request.
†John G. Switzer.

SERGEANTS.

Edward Wike, promoted 1st Sergeant, July 1, 1862.
Adolph Wolbrecht, reduced to ranks at his own request.
Carl H. Gramp, reduced to ranks at his own request.
Ferdinand Benz, reduced to ranks at his own request.
Robert Lang, appointed 1st Sergeant, September 30, 1862.
Curtis Michaelson, reduced to the ranks, March 23, 1864.
Andreas Oinhausen, appointed 1st Sergeant, November 14, 1863.
†Wm. Stober, appointed 1st Sergeant, April 18, 1865.
Emil Neese, appointed 1st Sergeant, July 1, 1864.
John G. Switzer, appointed 1st Sergeant, June 30, 1865.
John Van Raden, reduced to ranks, January 15, 1865.
†Alfred Berg.
†Anton Bauer.
†Wm. Keeren.

CORPORALS.

Albert Kocher, reduced to ranks, December 26, 1861.
Arnold Rader, reduced to ranks, January 16, 1862.
Carl Lipinsky, reduced to ranks, January 16, 1862.
John Oechxle, reduced to ranks, January 16, 1862.
Robert Lang, appointed Sergeant, November 10, 1861.
Curtis Michaelson, appointed Sergeant, January 16, 1862.
Emil Neese, reduced to ranks, January 16, 1862, re-appointed May 1, 186
Peter Steinmetz, reduced to ranks, January 16, 1862.
Anton Bauer, reduced to ranks January 16, 1862.
Heinrich Krumme, reduced to ranks, May 1, 1862.
Wm. Dobile, reduced to ranks, March 1, 1863.
Charles Latour, reduced to ranks, July 1, 1862.
Albert Polman, discharged, October 13, 1862.
Heinrich Klock, died of disease, July 4, 1862.
Johann Abels, reduced to ranks, May 1, 1862.
Phillip Vakopp, reduced to ranks, April 1, 1862.
Johann Esch, deserted, October 24, 1862.
Wm. Stober, appointed Sergeant, July 1, 1862.
John G. Switzer, appointed Sergeant, November 14, 1863.
John Van Raden, appointed Sergeant, March 23, 1864.
Johann Wolf, reduced to ranks at his own request, September 30, 1862.
Alfred Berg, appointed Sergeant, July 1, 1864.
Martin Byrne, reduced to ranks, March 23, 1864.
Wm. Heeren, appointed Sergeant, April 21, 1864.
†Friedrich Miller.
†Jacob Hoebel.
Henry A. Wernicke, reduced to ranks, August 1, 1865.
Frank Schroeder, discharged by order, 1865.
‡Phillip Friday.
†Anton Erchle.
†Christian Mensenkamp.
†Henry Cohlstedt.

PRIVATES.

†Arens Peter, veteran.
Abels Johann, mustered out September 13, 1864, expiration of term.
†Altman Henry.
†Adams George W., transferred from 99th Illinois Infantry.
Berg, Alfred, veteran, appointed Corporal, July 1, 1862.
Bauer Anton, veteran, appointed Corporal, December 26, 1861.
Byrne Martin, veteran, deserted December 31, 1865.
Benz Ferdinand, mustered out September 14, 1864, expiration of term.
Bockholder Jan, mustered out September 13, 1864, expiration of term.
Bonn Joseph, deserted October 24, 1862.
Bagger Heinrich, died of disease October 15, 1862.
Bies Albert, discharged G. O. No. 77 War Department.
†Burkhardt John.
†Backer Jacob.
Bender John L., mustered out May 22, 1865.
†Barmington Friedrich.
†Baker Jacob.
Brown John W., transferred to Company D, March 11, 1864.
Burkhardt Adolph, trans. from 11th Ill. Vol., died of disease August, 18
Cruse John, deserted October 24, 1862.
Cennes Friedrich, died January 7, 1865.
Cohlstedt Henry, appointed Corporal August 1, 1865.
Cruger Henry, died April 24, 1864.
†Christian John, transferred from 99th Illinois Infantry.
†Duitzman Wolbrand, vet.
‡Dobile Wilhelm, vet.
Denzing Friedrich, mustered out September 10, 1864, expiration of terr
‡Diller Michael, vet.
Dressman Uppo, deserted October 24, 1862.
‡Dede Henry.
‡Davis Phillip.
Dennis Thomas, transferred from 99th Ill. Inf., died of disease Dec., 186

Esh John, deserted October 24, 1862.
Eyhusen Brume W., died of disease May 19, 1863.
Eschel Anton, appointed Corporal March 1, 1865.
Froning Herman, discharged October 14, 1863.
Farley Thomas, transferred to Company K, March 1, 1862.
Frevort Friedrich, discharged January 12, 1862.
Frey John, died of disease July 5, 1863.
Frevert Charles, died of disease Dec. 19, 1864.
‡Friedman Valentine.
Friday Phillip, appointed Corporal Sept. 1, 1864.
‡Franz Safrin.
‡Fosler George.
Gramp Carl H., discharged Sept. 9, 1864—expiration of term.
Giboml Heinrich, killed April 6, 1862, at Shiloh.
Gressley Gottlieb, died of wounds received at Shiloh, April 26, 1862.
Garsteger Anton, deserted Dec. 31, 1865.
‡Getz Andrew.
Harberts Harbert, appointed 1st Sergeant Sept. 10, 1861.
Heeren Wm., vet., appointed Corporal March 23, 1864.
Hasselman Friedrich, killed at Shiloh, April 7, 1862.
Harberts Johann, discharged Feb. 4, 1863.
Husengo Ontje, died of disease, May 5, 1862.
†Hafmeiner Joseph.
†Hencke Wilhelm.
Hoebel Jacob, appointed Corporal March 23, 1864.
Heine Friedrich, killed July 7, 1864, battle Jackson Cross Roads.
†Held Friedrich.
†Jaeger John.
†Knoeller George, vet.
Kocher Albert, died of disease, May 15, 1862.
Kahn Conrad, died of disease, May 15, 1862.
Koeller Johann, discharged Sept. 9, 1864—expiration of term.
Kuhlmeir Heinrich, discharged Sept. 13, 1864—expiration of term.
Kraemer Falkert, died of disease, May 26, 1862.
Krueger Klaas, discharged Feb. 5, 1863.
Klock Heinrich, died of disease July 4, 1862.
Knock Andreas, killed at Shiloh April 6, 1862.
Kaumer Christian, discharged June 19, 1862.
Krumme Heinrich, transferred to Co. G, May 1, 1862.
†Koller Wm., vet.
†Kohle Jacob.
†Kohle Joseph.
†Kraemer George.
Kesterer John, died of disease, Sept. 18, 1864.
Krueger Carl, died of disease, Nov. 29, 1864.
†Kastler Niclaus.
†Kautenberger Peter G.
†Knecht Phillip.
†Kuhler August.
†Kogm Friedrich.
†Koehler Friedrich.
†Korm Louis.
†Koller Friedrich.
†Kraemer George W.
†Kleter George.
Lang Robert, appointed Corporal Sept. 10, 1861.
†Lipinsky Carl, vet., appointed Corporal Sept. 10, 1861.
†Latour Charles, vet., appointed Corporal Jan. 16, 1862.
Lapp Aaron, died of disease, March 4, 1862.
†Lahre John.
†Lahre Isaac.
†Ludicke Henry.
Liter Niclaus, discharged Oct. 8, 1865—term expired.
†Lahre Elias.
†Lang Charles M.
†Lang Jacob.
†Lubben Alexander.
Linemen Hey P., discharged Oct. 8, 1865—expiration of term of service.
Lang Richard, transferred from 99th Illinois Infantry.
March James, transferred to vet. Reserve Corps, Nov. 10, 1863.
Michaelson Curtis, deserted Oct. 1, 1864.
†Miller Gottfried, vet.
Metzger Richard, transferred to vet. Reserve Corps, Sept. 19, 1863.
Marbeth Leans, killed at Shiloh April 7, 1862.
Marks Jan F., killed at Shiloh April 6, 1862.
Marks Markus, discharged June 19, 1862.
Miller Friedrich, vet., appointed Corporal March 23, 1864.
†Miller William.
†Miller Right.
Miller Henry C., died of disease, Aug. 21, 1864.
Meise Conrad, drowned in Mississippi River Aug 24, 1864.
Mensinkam Christian P., appointed Corporal April 18, 1865.
Neese Emil, vet., appointed Corporal Sept. 10, 1861.

Neef Herman, discharged Sept. 13, 1864—expiration of term.
Neef Johann, discharged Dec. 4, 1862.
Ningen Jacob Van, discharged Nov. 12, 1864—expiration of term.
Oinhausen Andreas, vet., appointed Sergeant Jan. 16, 1862.
Olthoff Wilhelm, discharged Oct. 29, 1864—expiration of term.
Olthoff Anton, discharged Sept. 13, 1864—expiration of term.
Oechxle John, vet., appointed Corporal Sept. 10, 1861.
†Otto Charles.
O'Kannis Peter, died of disease, June 12, 1865.
†O'Kannis Cornelius.
Penning Wiard, died of disease, Dec. 31, 1861.
Polman Abett, discharged Oct. 13, 1862.
Persting Friedrich, discharged Sept. 13, 1864—expiration of term.
†Plumer Johann, vet.
†Pepperling Christoph vet.
†Prince Jacob.
Rader Arnold, vet., appointed Corporal March 23, 1864.
†Raden John Van, vet.
Rebel Johann, killed at Shiloh April 6, 1862.
Richeameir Conrad, died June 1, 1862, of wounds received at Shiloh.
†Rohrback Jacob.
†Romelfanger Jacob.
†Rach Ernst.
†Rippberger John.
†Reinicke Joseph.
†Restine George, transferred from 99th Illinois Vols.
Steinmetz Peter, vet., appointed Corporal Sept. 10, 1861—died October, 1864.
Stoecker Albert, discharged June 8, 1862.
Stober William, vet., appointed Corporal May 1, 1862.
Switzer John G., vet., appointed Corporal May 1, 1862.
†Stoehr John, vet.
Schneider Henry, discharged Dec. 11, 1862.
Schmalzhaf Heinrich, died April 24, 1862, of wounds received at Shiloh.
Stiefenhafer Martin, died of disease, June 25, 1862.
Steinhauer Jacob, discharged May 24, 1862.
Siedenburg Friedrich, discharged at Camp Butler.
Spiess Jacob, killed Oct. 4, 1862, at Hatchie.
Schraeder Frank, appointed Corporal March 23, 1864.
Schneider Joseph, deserted March 18, 1864.
†Schwarze Heinrich.
†Schmidt Johann.
Schlueker Henry, drowned Aug. 26, 1864.
Steffen Michael, discharged June 7, 1865.
†Stark Henry.
†Schroenstein Burkhardt.
†Streeger Peter.
Schroeder Charles, discharged June 7, 1865.
†Sauer Julius.
†Sieferman Lorenzo.
†Schneider Andrew C.
Trei Freidrich, died of disease, May 9, 1864.
†Trible Wilhelm.
Vakopp Philip, vet., died of disease, March 21, 1864.
Volmer Gottlieb, drowned in Mississippi River, May 14, 1863.
Wike Edward, appointed Sergeant Sept. 10, 1861.
Wolbrecht Adolph, discharged Sept. 13, 1863, to receive promotion.
Weifenbach John, discharged July 24, 1862.
†Weggenhausen Max, vet.
†Wolff Johann, vet.
†Wernicke Henry A.
†Wagner Herman L.
†Wike Louis.
Wunderlin Savoir, discharged May 26, 1865.
Wiarda Theodore, deserted Dec. 31, 1865.
†Weiner Jacob.
†Wepel Hemme.
†Wagner Wilhelm.
Ziebrich Paulres, discharged Nov. 23, 1862.

COMPANY "D."

FIRST ORGANIZATION.

CAPTAIN.

Wm. F. Wilder, resigned November 24th, 1862.

1st LIEUTENANT.

Joel L. Coe, resigned November 24th, 1862.

2d LIEUTENANT.
Henry H. Woodbury, appointed Adjutant March 2d, 1863.

1st SERGEANTS.
Jasper M. Cadmus, died of disease May 6th, 1862.
Uriah J. Terry.*

SERGEANTS.
Everett Rollins, discharged November 24th, 1862.
Uriah J. Terry, appointed 1st Sergeant.
Andrew F. Echelberger, killed at Shiloh, April 7, 1862.
Hial Pike, discharged April 21st, 1862.
James W. Holmes.*
Edwin S. Hubbard, died at La Grange, Tenn., July 5, 1862.
Harlan P. Forbes,* reduced to ranks at his own request, 1862.

CORPORALS.
Frank Howard.*
John Trowbridge, died of disease March 12, 1862.
Charles S. Beebe.*
Eugene T. Thomas.*
James W. Holmes, appointed Sergeant.
Joel P. Keyes, discharged to accept promotion in U. S. C. I., 1863.
Geo. W. Manning, died at Keokuk, Iowa, August 21, 1862, of wounds received at Shiloh.
Edwin S. Hubbard, appointed Sergeant.

MUSICIANS.
Nathan Sanborn, discharged October 7, 1862.
Walter Sanborn, discharged June 25, 1862.

PRIVATES.
Angier Abel, discharged December 5, 1862.
Angier Leander, died of disease, Sept. 21, 1862, at Memphis, Tenn.
Alexander Christopher C., died of disease April 21, 1862, at Cincinnatti.
Ash George, killed at Shiloh, April 6, 1862.
Burrington John, died of disease at Amboy, Ill., June 6, 1862.
Bixby David, discharged November 4, 1862.
Butterfield Gilbert L., transferred to Mulligan's Irish Brigade.
Bird Roderick D.*
Barnard George S.*
Bradbury Eben C.*
Benjamin Porter.*
Balmer James, discharged November 24, 1862, at Bolivar, Tenn.
Crocker Freeman F., discharged July 12, 1862.
Cromwell Daniel.*
Clark Daniel, discharged November 24, 1862.
Crane Thomas S.*
Crawford Samuel E., died of disease.
Case Franklin, discharged October 8, 1862.
Conoway John, discharged April 28, 1862.
Dexter John, discharged July 10, 1862.
Dow John W.*
Donnovan Dennis.*
Echelberger Benjamin P.*
Fenstermaker Tillman, died of disease May 2, 1862, at Shiloh.
Forbes Harlan,* appointed Sergeant ―――, 1862.
Graves Aspasia.*
Harmon James.*
Holmes Jacob L., discharged October 11, 1862.
Holton Jerome R.*
Howarter Henry E., discharged September 4, 1862.
Hill Truman, died of disease, October 22, 1862, at Bolivar, Tenn.
Hoxie Oscar, died at Pittsburg Landing, April 2, 1862.
Kipley Lorenzo.*
Lovering Leonard, died near Corinth, May 28th, 1862.
Lovering Henry, died near Corinth, June 5, 1862.
Larish Almon S.*
Lasher George.*
Mulligan Jacob W.*
Millard Samuel, killed at Shiloh, April 6, 1862.
Morse Benjamin W.*
Madden John.*
Myers James.*
Melley James, killed at Shiloh, April 7, 1862.
McCarty John, died of wounds received at Shiloh.
Morris David.*
Morris John A.*
Miller Jacob P.*
Manchester Lewis M.*
Myer Henry, discharged April 21, 1862.
Merchant Myron V., transfered H Company.
Nunn Robert.*

Post Jacob.*
Parsons Nelson, discharged April 1st, 1862.
Roff Clark P.*
Ritz Martin L.*
Smith John, discharged December 5, 1862, at St. Louis.
Stevens Burrell, died May 4, 1862, at Shiloh.
Sausman John L., discharged June 11, 1862.
Sanson Oliver.*
Sweet Josiah B., killed at Shiloh April 6, 1862.
Smith James P., died at Fairhaven, Ill., June 23, 1862.
Tearney Edward.*
Whiting Henry B.*
Whiting John F., discharged July 18, 1862, of wounds received at Shiloh.
Whiting Charles L., deserted January, 1863.
Wales Martin, missing in action at Shiloh, supposed to be dead.
Woolsey Philander H.*
Waterhouse Lewis, died at Pittsburg Landing, March 20, 1862.
Winebremer John B.*
Wood Wm. H., died at St. Louis, May 27, 1862, of disease.
Windle Wm., discharged August 4, 1862.
Wier Thomas.*
Wressell David.*

*Company D was assigned to duty in Company I, November 2d, 1862, by order of Col. B. Dornblazer, commanding Regiment, and was consolidated with Company I March 2d, 1863, by General Order No. 8, State of Illinois. All men marked with an asterisk, thus (*), were transferred to Company I as above.

COMPANY "D."

NEW ORGANIZATION.

CAPTAINS.

James W. Crane, left the service, April 7, 1865.
Francis O. Miller.

1st LIEUTENANTS.

Francis O. Miller, promoted Captain, June 6, 1865.
†Isaac Bobb.

2d LIEUTENANTS.

Isaac Bobb, promoted 1st Lieutenant, June 6, 1865.
†Benjamin F. Hayhurst.

1st SERGEANTS.

John P. Waggoner, reduced to ranks, June 15, 1864.
Benjamin F. Hayhurst, promoted to 2d Lieutenant, July 12, 1865.
†John Stine.

SERGEANTS.

Lansing Eells, killed May 14, 1864, near Vaughn's Station, Miss.
Andrew J. Bates, discharged February 14, 1865.
Michael Eshelman, reduced to ranks October 1, 1864, at his own request.
†Brayton Gardner.
†Robert A. Jones.
†Richard W. Hurlbut, vet.
·†Wm. Parker.
Benjamin F. Hayhurst, promoted to 1st Sergeant June 15, 1864.
John Stine, promoted to 1st Sergeant, July 12, 1865.

CORPORALS.

Richard W. Hurlbut, vet., reduced to ranks May 1, 1864.
Michael Eshelman, appointed Sergeant June 30, 1864.
Brayton Gardner, appointed Sergeant June 30, 1864.
Robert A. Jones, appointed Sergeant October 1, 1864.
Wm. Parker, appointed Sergeant July 12, 1865.
Levi Cross, reduced to ranks January 12, 1865, at his own request.
Jacob Winner, reduced to ranks June 1, 1865.
†Wm. W. Felt.
†Charles Caide.
†Michael Rogers.
John Brown, reduced to ranks January 1st, 1866.
John J. Aurand, discharged June 22d, 1865.
†Wm. Warren.
†John P. Waggoner.
†Joel Fry.

PRIVATES.

Aurand John J., appointed Corporal October 1, 1864.
†Addams John H., vet.
†Atkins Lewis E.

†Avery Wm. N.
Brenner Benjamin, died of disease July 2, 1864.
†Bollck Henry.
†Benton Levi.
†Brown James E.
†Boyer George.
†Belding Arthur.
†Bently Wm. M.
†Bently Lewis D.
†Beck John.
†Bundy Ambrose A.
†Bundy Christopher.
†Bistline Daniel.
†Brown John A., transferred from Company C March 11, 1864.
Brady Frederick, mustered out October, 1865, expiration of term.
Bates Andrew J., appointed Sergeant January 12, 1864.
†Berwick Augustus W., transferred from 99th Ill. Infantry.
†Brown Wm. W.
Cutting Henry P., transferred to vet. res. corps, April 24, 1865.
†Clark Wm. H.
†Clark Charles B.
†Clark John.
Calde Charles, appointed Corporal May 1, 1864.
†Calde Levi.
†Cook Sherman.
Bross Levi, appointed Corporal January 12, 1864.
†Daughenbaugh Jonathan.
†Denton Levi.
†Diemer Levi.
†Dunnegan Dennis.
†Edgar Wm.
Elster Daniel W., deserted August 20, 1864.
Eells Lansing, vet., appointed Sergeant January 12, 1864.
Eshelman Michael, appointed Corporal January 12, 1864.
Fiss Thomas J., discharged at Mobile, April, 1865.
Fogle John D., discharged September 28, 1864.
Frey Joel, appointed Corporal July 1, 1865.
†Fetzer Christian.
†Flory John.
Felt Wm. W., appointed Corporal January 12, 1864.
†Furray Wm.
†Gressenger Wm.
†Grinnel Wm. D.
Gardner Brayton, appointed Corporal January 12, 1864.
†Gross Theodore.
Hayhurst Benjamin F., vet., appointed Sergeant January 12, 1864.
Hayden Luther H., died of disease January 5, 1865.
†Hammond Marvin.
Hurlbut Richard W., vet., appointed Corporal January 12, 1864, appointed Sergeant March 1, 1865.
Johnson James W., discharged at Mobile, April, 1865.
Jones Robert A., appointed Corporal January 12, 1864.
†Kleckner John P.
†Kleckner Jacob.
†Kahley Joseph.
†Keller Henry.
†King Henry.
Knight Hiram, died of disease June 3, 1864.
Keohler Christian, deserted November, 1865.
†Keohler John.
Lincoln Albert, discharged July 7, 1865.
†Lighthart Warren H.
†Lee Samuel.
†Leverton Isaac.
†Lultz Wm.
†Lenart Elias.
†Melton Leonard L.
†Minick Nathaniel.
†Musser John W.
†Musser Raymond.
†Morehouse Warren E.
†McGellegan Wm. K.
†McGellegan Joseph.
Maxwell Joseph W., died of disease August 23, 1864.
†Mattingly James.
Messenger George W., discharged May 31, 1865.
†Messenger Wm.
Mudy George W., died of disease October 19, 1864.
†Machamar Aaron.
†Manin Samuel, transferred from 99th Illinois Infantry.
Parker Wm., appointed Corporal January 1st, 1864.
†Pangborn George E.
†Plummer Jerome B.

†Rush Joseph.
†Rush Emanuel.
Reed James H., transferred to Company E, March 8, 1865.
†Reed Stephen A.
†Randall James.
Rogers Michael, appointed Corporal June 30, 1864.
Rudle Jacob, died of disease July 5, 1865.
Spitler Wm. H., appointed Corporal July 12, 1865.
Solace Chester L., deserted October, 1865.
†Shumaker John A.
†Scrambling Wm. H.
†Spofford Charles F.
Stine John, appointed Sergeant January 12, 1864.
Sincox Allison, died August 5, 1865.
†Towle Henry E.
Tyler Dayton D., vet., transferred from Company B, March 8, 1865, discharged November, 1865, War Department order.
†Tucker James, transferred from 99th Illinois Infantry.
†Tanksley Wm. A., transferred from 99th Illinois Infantry.
Vaughn Oscar O., deserted October, 1865.
†Verguson John S.
Vance Orrin C., deserted October, 1865.
†Williams James E.
Warren Wm., appointed Corporal Januaay 13, 1865.
†Whittenmyer John H.
Waggoner John P., appointed Sergeant January 12, 1864, appointed Corporal June 1, 1865.
Winner Jacob, appointed Corporal Jan. 12, 1864, dishonorably discharged.
†Young Wm.
†Zerby Jacob.

COMPANY "E."

CAPTAINS.

John M. Marble, dismissed the service Aug. 8, 1864, by order Sec. of War.
†Frederick H. Marsh.

1st LIEUTENANTS.

Wm. Lane, discharged for disability Sept. 11, 1862.
Frederick H. Marsh, promoted Captain Nov. 2, 1864.
†Wm. N. Haney.

2d LIEUTENANTS.

Wm. A. Plantz, resigned May 23, 1862.
Albert Selzick, resigned July 11, 1864.
†Samuel V. Boyer.

1st SERGEANTS.

Henry A. Briggs, discharged Aug. 15, 1862, of wounds received in action.
Frederick H. Marsh, promoted to 1st Lieut. Sept. 11, 1862.
Wilson S. Lenhart, discharged Dec. 1, 1864.
Samuel V. Boyer, promoted 2d Lieut. May 25, 1865.
†Bela T. St. John.

SERGEANTS.

Frederick H. Marsh, appointed 1st Sergeant Aug. 15, 1862.
Wilson S. Lenhart, appointed 1st Sergeant Oct, 21, 1862.
John Reimer, transferred to veteran reserve corps, March 25, 1864.
Wm. N. Haney, promoted to 1st Lieut. Nov. 24, 1864.
†David Evans.
Wm. Morton, died of disease, June 6, 1862.
†Joseph R. Gibson.
Samuel V. Boyer, appointed 1st Sergeant Dec. 1, 1864.
†Elliot E. Pollard.
Samuel Roberts, discharged May 20, 1862.
†Samuel Evans.

CORPORALS.

John McClintock, died of disease, Oct. 16, 1862.
Joseph Boyles, discharged Dec. 25, 1862.
Elliot E. Pollard, appointed Sergeant Dec. 1, 1865.
†Henry H. Bemis.
Samuel L. Evans, appointed Sergeant March 1, 1865.
†Wm. F. Linsley.
James F. Jackson, discharged May 5, 1862.
Joseph R. Gibson, appointed Sergeant April 4, 1864.
Isaiah Davey, discharged Dec. 1, 1864.
†Elmore G. Titus.

David Evans, appointed Sergeant, Dec. 1, 1864.
Bela T. St. John, reduced to ranks at his own request, July 22, 1863.
†John T. Boyer.
Frederick A. Andrews, reduced to ranks at his own request, July 10, 1862.
Samuel V. Boyer, promoted Sergeant Oct. 16, 1862.
Joseph R. Kennedy, died Sept. 9, 1863.
†Lafayette J. Justis.
George O. Cooper, reduced to ranks at his request, Oct. 29, 1864.
Thomas Aurner, reduced to ranks at his own request, July 15, 1865.
†Benjamin Switzer.
†Charles W. Roberts.
†James R. Shultz.

PRIVATES.

Auner Porter, discharged Dec. 9, 1862.
Austin Charles E., transferred from 11th Illinois Infantry—mustered out expiration of term, Oct. 7, 1865.
Andrews Frederick A., appointed Corporal Dec. 1, 1861—died of disease January 31, 1864.
Auner Thomas, vet., appointed Corporal March 1, 1865.
Bosley Julius, vet., deserted Dec. 1, 1865.
Birdsell Charles H., transferred to vet. Reserve Corps, Nov. 10, 1863.
Blodgett Douglass, died of disease, March 6, 1862.
†Boyer John T., vet.
†Bemus Henry H., vet.
†Benjamin Harvey L., vet.
†Buckley Warren E.
†Butler James.
Burk John, transferred from 11th Illinois Infantry—mustered out Oct. 7 1865—expiration of term.
†Brassel Thomas, transferred from 11th Illinois Infantry.
†Buckley Morrill.
Cooper George O., appointed Corporal May 5, 1862—discharged Dec. 1, 1864.
Cole James M., vet., deserted Dec. 31, 1865.
Creighton Henry, died of disease, July 13, 1862.
Cowell John W., died in Southern prison, May 7, 1862.
Carpenter Ralph L., died of disease Jan. 19, 1865.
Cassady John, deserted Jan. 1, 1866.
†Colcord Albert H.
†Colcord Ivory A.
†Callender James, transferred from 99th Illinois Infantry.
Dodge Columbus, died of disease May 4, 1862.
Davey Isaiah, appointed Corporal Oct. 29, 1862,
Demuth Frederick, discharged Aug. 9, 1865.
Eades Jonathan, died of disease, May 12, 1862.
Evans Samuel L., vet., appointed Corporal April 4, 1864.
†Evans Columbus D.
Frazier David, deserted May 13, 1863.
Frank John F., died of disease, June 10, 1862.
Fuller Abram B., discharged Sept. 28, 1862.
French James W., vet., died on Steamer Planet, Jan. 19, 1864.
†Ferguson Russel L.
Gillespie Peter, vet., transferred to K Co., February 29, 1864.
Gurley Isaiah, transferred from 11th Illinois Infantry—discharged for disability, July, 1865.
Hays David, died of disease, April, 19, 1862.
Hill Jesse, discharged Aug. 15, 1862.
Haney Wm. N., vet., appointed Sergeant July 1, 1862.
Hopkins Wm. T., discharged Dec. 25, 1862.
Hodges Jesse G., discharged Dec. 1, 1864.
Holden John, discharged Nov. 12, 1862.
Hill James, discharged May 25, 1862.
†Hall Wm. J.
†Hammond Andrew J.
Imlay Robert, vet., killed at battle Jackson, Miss., July 7, 1864.
†Johnston Gustavus, vet.
†Johnston August, vet.
Justus Lafayette, vet., appointed Corporal April 4, 1864.
Johnston Wm. W., deserted Dec. 31, 1865.
†Junior Alexander, transferred from 11th Illinois Infantry.
Kennedy Joseph R., died of disease Sept. 9, 1863.
†Koln John W.
†Keenan Michael.
Lenhart Silas N., died of disease, May 2, 1862.
Laidley David, discharged Sept. 29, 1862.
Lathrop Carlo, died of disease, May 4, 1862.
Longedon Rufus, deserted Dec. 19, 1862.
Lindsay Wm. E., vet. appointed Corporal April 4, 1864.
Larry Hiram, deserted Nov. 4, 1864.
†Law John W.
†Leslie Edward.
†Long Isaac.
McNeil Alexander, discharged Dec. 1, 1864—expiration of term.
†Morton John, vet.

Martin James S., died of disease, May 16, 1862.
†Mann Frank, vet.
Marble Roscoe, deserted May 13, 1863.
†Moxley Risdon R., vet.
McGee Mathew, discharged Sept. 5, 1862.
McCloud David, died of disease, April 4, 1862.
Mellenger John B., discharged Nov. 11, 1862.
Middaugh John E., deserted July 16, 1864.
†Moshier Lorenzo.
†Marian Joseph.
†Moses Lewis.
Moses Wm. M., discharged Oct. 9, 1865—War Department order, No. 77.
McGinness Chester, transferred from 11th Illinois Infantry—mustered out expiration of term, Oct. 4, 1865.
†Mullnaux John, transferred from 11th Illinois Infantry.
Newton James, discharged Dec. 1, 1864.
Noble Alonzo B., deserted Nov. 18, 1863.
Newton Addison, discharged Sept. 29, 1862.
†O'Neil Patrick, vet.
†O'Brien Patrick, vet.
†Palmer Wm., vet.
Pearl Joseph, died of disease, June 27, 1863.
Peck Charles W., died of disease, July 19, 1863.
†Plantz Victor A., vet.
‡Pike Thomas.
‡Peaslee Cornelius.
‡Phillips Christopher.
Phillips Wm. H., deserted Jan. 2, 1866.
Patterson Orrin, transferred from 11th Illinois Infantry—mustered out expiration of term, Oct., 1865.
Plank Christian, transferred from 11th Illinois Infantry.
Quinn Edward, deserted Oct. 12, 1865.
Remer John, appointed Sergeant July 1, 1862.
Ryan Michael, vet., discharged for disability, June, 1865.
‡Russell Alanson H., vet.
Roberts Charles W., appointed Corporal March 1, 1865.
‡Randall Willis A.
‡Root Samuel H., transferred from I Co., June 10, 1865.
‡Roadnight Wm. H., vet,
‡Runkle John S.
Rishel John G., discharged May 27, 1865.
‡Reed Isaac W.
Reed James H., transferred from D Co., March 8, 1865.
Roper Allen P., vet., transferred from 11th Illinois Infantry.
Ransford Henry, transferred from 11th Illinois Infantry—mustered out expiration of term, Sept. 30, 1865.
Selzick Albert, promoted 2d Lieut. July 3, 1862.
Switzer Benjamin, vet., appointed Corporal March 1, 1865.
Sheehy Michael, deserted March 18, 1863.
* St. John Bela T., vet., appointed Corporal Aug. 16, 1862—appointed 1st Sergeant Sept. 1, 1865.
Smith James P., discharged Nov. 10, 1862.
Shultz James R., vet., appointed Corporal July 15, 1865.
Simmers Mathias, discharged dec 4, 1862, of wounds received at Shiloh.
Still John, discharged May 5, 1862.
Swanson Peter, vet., discharged March 15, 1865.
‡Steele David.
‡Shaw Wm.
‡Shaw Stephen.
‡Stonebraker Jasper N.
Shumake John, died from effects of stab of knife at Natchitoches, La., Aug. 15, 1865.
Stonebraker Ellphalet J., mustered out expiration of term, Oct. 17, 1865.
Springer David, discharged May 27, 1865.
‡Shaw Wm. E.
‡Seyler Peter.
‡Saxby Wm. R.
‡Sidles Charles Z.
Shaw John W., vet., transferred from 11th Illinois Infantry—deserted July 8, 1865.
Spears Henry, transferred from 11th Illinois Infantry—deserted July 8, 1865.
†Trefethen Alfred M., vet.
Thompson Henry, discharged Nov. 12, 1862.
Titus Elmore Y., vet., appointed Corporal April 4, 1864.
Tilton Horace, discharged Nov. 10, 1862.
Turney Robert W., died of disease, Oct. 20, 1864.
‡Trenholm Robert.
‡Trenholm John W.
Thorp Isaac N., drowned Jan. 3, 1865.
‡Trotter James, transferred from A Co., March 17, 1864.
‡Tozer Alonzo, transferred from 99th Illinois Infantry.
Vennum Edward C., discharged March 30, 1863.
‡Wheeler Wm. N., vet.

Welsh Peter, died of disease, May 4, 1862.
Wilber John T. S., died of disease, May 13, 1863.
Wetherbee Ephraim, transferred to vet. reserve corps. March 26, 1864.
White Wm. J., discharged June 14, 1865.
White Chas, O., died of wounds received at battle of Jackson, Miss., July 22, 1864.
Wilson Albert, discharged July 16, 1864.
Waddell Wm. W., transferred to A Co., Sept. 1, 1865.
Wright James, transferred from 11th Illinois Infantry—mustered out expiration of term, Oct. 4, 1865.
Weddell Jesse R., transferred from 11th Illinois Infantry, died Aug. 3, 1865.

COMPANY "F."

CAPTAINS.

Thomas Wakefield, mustered out Dec. 29th, 1864, expiration of term.
†Francis M. Lollar.

1st LIEUTENANTS.

John W. Barr, discharged March 20th, 1864, to accept promotion in 6th U. S. C. Artillery.
John Shaw, mustered out Dec. 29th, 1864, expiration of term.
†Alvin T. Byrne.

2d LIEUTENANTS.

Winfield S. Ingraham, died April 23d, 1862, of wounds received at Shiloh.
John Shaw, promoted to 1st Lieutenant, April 21st, 1862.
Francis M. Lollar, promoted to Captain March 20th, 1865.
†John L. Carter.

1st SERGEANTS.

Jesse B. Shadle, reduced to ranks March 21, 1865.
John Shaw, promoted to 2d Lieutenant Dec. 26, 1862.
Wm. W. Crosson, reduced to Sergeant Jan. 15, 1863.
Francis M. Lollar, promoted to 2d Lieutenant July 24, 1864.
Alexander R. Barker, vet., discharged Sept. 9, 1864.
Alvin T. Byrne, promoted to 1st Lieutenant March 20, 1860.
†Wm. W. Crosson, vet.

SERGEANTS.

Eli Crouse, mustered out June 19th, 1865, expiration of term.
George Elder, discharged December 12, 1862.
George W. Orman, died of disease July 20, 1862.
Jesse B. Shadle, discharged Dec. 31, 1863, to receive promotion in colored organization.
George A. White, discharged July 9. 1862.
Alexander R. Barker, appointed 1st Sergeant July 24, 1864.
Jonathan Blair, died of disease August 24, 1862.
Francis M. Lollar, appointed 1st Sergeant Jan. 13, 1863.
Calvin Crouse, discharged June 2, 1862.
Alvin T. Byrne, appointed 1st Sergeant September 10, 1864.
†Charles Boyd, veteran.
†Andrew J. Shores.
†Milton Wakefield, vet.
John L. Carter, promoted to 2d Lieutenant, April 9, 1865.
Wm. W. Crosson, appointed 1st Sergeant March 20, 1865.
†Hays Wm., transferred from 11th Illinois Infantry.
†Samuel T. Beddo, transferred from 11th Ill. Inf., reduced to ranks July 5, 1865.

CORPORALS.

Aaron D. Shadle, discharged November 7, 1862.
Quinton J. Bryant, died of disease June 7, 1862.
John L. Carter, appointed Sergeant February 28, 1864.
Joshua F. Harlow, discharged March 5, 1863.
Wm. W. Crosson, appointed Sergeant January 15, 1863.
James F. Brotherton, reduced to ranks March 26, 1864.
Milton Wakefield, vet., appointed Sergeant September 10, 1864.
Lot S. Rogers, died of disease June 30, 1862.
George W. Ridman, vet., reduced to ranks March 20, 1864.
†Walter P. Daniel.
Zimori C. Witzman, reduced to ranks May 9, 1865, mustered out June 19, 1865, expiration of term.
†David Reeves, vet.
†Wm. L. Wakefield, vet.
Wm. H. Littler, vet., reduced to ranks at his own request July 16, 1864.
†James Miller, vet.
James S. Jackson, died of disease October 10, 1864.

Samuel McGuire, mustered out June 19, 1865, expiration of term.
Charles Boyd, appointed Sergeant March 20, 1865.
†Joshua Arnold.
Ephraim M. Bryan, reduced to ranks.
Hooper C. Morgan, died of disease September 27, 1862.
†Wm. A. Wood.
Eli Crouse appointed Sergeant July 24, 1864.
Erhard Stoll, reduced to ranks at his own request.
†Joseph Cradler, vet., transferred from 11th Illinois Infantry.
†August Rump, vet., transferred from 11th Illinois Infantry.

PRIVATES.

†Abbott James P., discharged April 7, 1862, re-enlisted January 14, 1864.
Arnold Joshua, vet., appointed Corporal March 20, 1865.
†Acres Wm. W.
†Anderson James P., transferred from 11th Illinois Infantry.
Boyd Charles, vet., appointed Corporal July 24, 1864.
Barker Alexander R., vet., appointed Sergeant May 1, 1862.
†Bryan Wm., vet.
Ballard Henry C., died of disease October 22, 1862.
Bryan Wm. H., died of wounds received at Shiloh, April 25, 1862.
Bryan Ephraim M., appointed Corporal August, 1862, mustered out Dec. 29 1864.
Bryant Richard R., discharged February 15, 1863.
†Brant Johnson W., vet.
Brown Harrison, discharged August 20, 1862.
Byrne Alvin T., vet., appointed Sergeant August, 1862.
Barnett James W., died of disease August 8, 1863.
Brooks Jonathan, discharged May 13, 1865.
Babbitt Francis C., died of disease November 9, 1864.
†Behymer Thomas, vet.
Brotherton James F., appointed Corporal December 29, 1861, transferred to vet. res. corps March 26, 1864.
Bixler Hiram, died of disease February 17, 1864.
Butroff John, died of disease November 24, 1864.
†Broms Lamus, transferred from 11th Ill. Infantry.
Blair Ransom, transferred from 11th Ill. Inf., mustered out October, 1865, expiration of term.
†Blanchard James, transferred from 11th Ill. Infantry.
†Beddoe Samuel T., transferred from 11th Ill. Infantry.
Blair Jonathan, appointed Sergeant December 29, 1861.
Bryant Quintin J., appointed Corporal December 29, 1861.
†Craig Joshua B., vet., discharged August 28, 1862, re-enlisted Dec. 29, 1863.
Crowse Calvin, appointed Sergeant March 31, 1862.
Crowse Eli, appointed Corporal February 29, 1864.
Chrissman Benj. F., mustered out Dec. 29, 1864, expiration of term.
Clark Riley, discharged May 3, 1862.
Corder John J., died of disease June 12, 1862.
Craig John W., died of disease December 8, 1861.
Clark John W., died of disease August 5, 1862.
Carter Parkson, died of disease September 1, 1863.
†Cravens Henry H., vet.
Carter Robert M., mustered out December 29, 1864, expiration of term.
†Covell Thomas G., vet.
Chrisman Silas, died of disease August 26, 1864.
Chapman James H., died June, 1865.
Curtis Elmsly, mustered out May 18, 1865, War Department order.
†Carter Thomas.
Crosson Wm. W., appointed Corporal December 29, 1861.
Carter John L., appointed Corporal December 29, 1861.
Caughlin Thomas, transferred from 11th Ill. Inf., mustered out October, 1865, expiration of term.
†Curney Samuel, transferred from 99th Illinois Infantry.
Daniel Walter P., vet., appointed Corporal March 29, 1864.
Devore David J., died of disease July 22, 1862.
†DeJaynes Lewis, transferred from 99th Illinois Infantry.
†Ernst Joel C., vet.
Elliott Wm., died of disease June 25, 1865.
†Ezzell Wm. J., transferred from 99th Illinois Infantry.
Elder George W., appointed Sergeant December 29, 1861.
Foster Henry R., mustered out December 29, 1864, expiration of term.
†Foreman Hugh L.
Gard Wm. F., died of disease November 4, 1864.
†Gard Mitchell.
†Gard Jarrett.
Gard George W., died of disease September, 1865.
†Gross Josiah.
‡Gettich Aaron.
Gleason James E., transferred from 11th Ill. Inf., mustered out October, 1865, expiration of term.
Gleason James, transferred from 11th Ill. Inf., mustered out October, 1865, expiration of term.
Harlow Joshua F., appointed Corporal December 29, 1861.
†Horsman Frederick, transferred from 11th Illinois Infantry.

Houston George W., transferred from 11th Ill. Infantry, mustered out October, 1865, expiration of term.
†Havie John, transferred from 11th Ill. Infantry.
Hart Henry C., vet., mustered out October, 1865, expiration of term.
†Hart John W.
Hanna Aaron, died of disease February 15, 1865.
†Heady Thomas S., vet.
Harris Levi, died of disease—date unknown.
Hinman Benj. L., mustered out December 29, 1864, expiration of term.
Hays Thomas, mustered out December 29, 1864, expiration of term.
Hinds Daniel T., discharged August 15, 1862.
Hellman Martin, transferred to V. R. C., September 19, 1863.
Hays James, deserted May 15, 1862.
†Haeuszler Conrad.
†Hitchcoock Frederick.
‡Hays Samuel P., transferred from 11th Illinois Infantry.
Hanifin Wm., transferred from 11th Illinois Infantry, mustered out October, 1865, expiration of term.
Ingraham Wm. I., died of disease February 3, 1864.
Ingraham Doman, transferred to V. R. C., March 26, 1864.
Jackson James S., appointed Corporal September 20, 1864.
Jones Thomas R., died of disease April 28, 1864.
‡Kelley John, transferred from 11th Illinois Infantry.
†Kimberlin Wm. O.
Knowles James M., died of disease December 15, 1861.
Knowles James R., died of disease May, 1862.
Kittle George, died of disease December 15, 1861.
†Littler Wm. H., vet., appointed Corporal February 29, 1864.
†Lyons James W.
Lear John W., died of disease February 20, 1864.
Lacey Caner, died of disease March 20, 1864.
†Lansing James, transferred from 11th Illinois Infantry.
Little Ira G., discharged, date unknown.
Logan Wm. S., died April 25, 1862, of wounds received at Shiloh.
Lollar Francis M., appointed Sergeant November 1, 1862.
†Mervin Patrick H., vet.
McGuire, Samuel, appointed Corporal July 10, 1864.
McCullum Stephen, died of disease August 6, 1864.
Montgomery James F., discharged May 3, 1862.
Miller James, vet., appointed Corporal February 29, 1864.
Morgan Hooper C., appointed Corporal August, 1862.
Marshall Squire, died of disease May 20, 1862.
†Manning Elisha, vet.
McKinney Robert P., died of disease June 3, 1862.
Mallory James C., transferred from Co. K. died of disease April 10, 1862.
Mahalfand Adam, discharged August 15, 1862.
Marshall James R., died of disease May 17, 1862.
†McMillen James.
Miller Crawford C., died of disease November 16, 1861.
McCaw Samuel M., mustered out August 1865, War Department order.
McClure Franklin, died of disease, date unknown.
Murphy James, died of disease February 22, 1864.
Moore Samuel B., deserted August 30, 1865, never reported to regiment.
McGhee Daniel, transferred from 11th Illinois Infantry, mustered out October 5, 1865, expiration of term.
Menzies Robert, transferred from 11th Illinois Infantry, mustered out October 5, 1865, expiration of term.
Nash Roswell, transferred from 11th Illinois Infantry, mustered out October 7, 1865, expiration of term.
Nichols Ira, transferred from 11th Illinois Infantry, mustered out October 7, 1865, expiration of term.
Oaster Benjamin, transferred to V. R. C., November 10, 1863.
†Otto Simon.
Oaster John, died of disease December 3, 1864.
Orman George W., appointed Sergeant December 29, 1861.
Pruett Walter P., discharged April 9, 1862.
†Phillips David C.
Pettey Stephen, transferred from 11th Illinois Infantry, mustered out October, 1865, expiration of term.
†Read Daniel.
†Read Nathaniel.
Read Franklin, died of disease January 14, 1864.
Rodeffer Wm. H. H., died of disease May 31, 1865.
†Runyan Bascom.
Rogers Wm. B., died of disease January 10, 1864.
Rude James, vet., died of disease July 21, 1864.
†Redman George W., vet., appointed Corporal November 7, 1862.
Rolfe Thomas E., mustered out December 29, 1865, expiration of term.
Rominger Franklin L., mustered out June 2d, 1865, expiration of term.
Rominger Oliver H., deserted December 19, 1865.
Reeves David, vet., appointed Corporal February 29, 1864.
Reid John, transferred from 11th Illinois Infantry, mustered out October, 1865, expiration of term.

Rogers Lott S., appointed Corporal December 29, 1861.
†Stewart John.
Stewart John W., died July 30, 1864, of wounds received at Jackson, Miss.
Self Josephus, vet., died of disease December 15, 1864.
Strawn Wm. F., vet., discharged May 30, 1865.
†Stewart Wm. R., vet.
Stock Wm., died of disease January 13, 1863.
Stoll Erhard, vet., appointed Corporal February 20, 1864, died of disease December 22, 1864.
†Stanley John C., vet.
†Schuler Frederick, vet.
†Stoll Frederick.
Smith Barney, died of disease, December 13, 1864.
†Staniford John H.
†Staniford George W.
Shore Andrew J., appointed Sergeant April 8, 1865.
†Shore Francis M.
Sanford Wm. H., deserted January 3d, 1866.
†Slaughter Joseph H.
Shadle Jesse B., appointed Sergeant August, 1862.
Shadle Aaron D., appointed Corporal December 29, 1861.
Stewart Geo. H., mustered out May 31, 1865, War Department order.
Toliver Francis M., died of disease April 1st, 1864.
†Truitt Alfred L.
†Taylor James A.
Taylor Stephen, died of disease December 14, 1861.
†Utterback John T.
Utterback Menville T., died of disease June 1, 1862.
Wood Wm. A., appointed Corporal October 29, 1864.
†Wells John.
†Wells Joseph P.
Woods James G., discharged November 23, 1862.
West Willis, discharged December 24, 1862.
Wakefield John, mustered out December 29, 1864, expiration of term.
Wakefield Wm. L., vet., appointed Corporal April, 1864.
Wakefield Milton, vet., appointed Corporal December 29, 1861.
†Weaver John G., vet.
†Weaver George W., vet.
White Reuben M., vet., killed by lightning March 15, 1865.
Wells Jefferson T., discharged May 28, 1862.
Witzman Zimri C., appointed Corporal April 1, 1863, mustered out June 19, 1865.
Wright James B., appointed Q. M. Sergeant, transferred to non-commissioned staff April 4, 1864.
‡Wright Reuben.
‡Wheeler Michael J.
†Walker James, transferred from 11th Illinois Infantry.
Wilcox Wm. B., transferred from 11th Illinois Infantry, mustered out October, 1865, expiration of term.
†Wood Thomas, transferred from 11th Illinois Infantry.
Wilson David B., transferred from 11th Illinois Infantry, mustered out May 13, 1865, expiration of term.
White George A., appointed Sergeant December 29, 1861.
*Weaver Isaac.

COMPANY "G."

CAPTAINS.

Wm. Young, resigned April 12, 1863.
Robert Smith, mustered out December 28, 1864, expiration of term.
Sam'l Buchanan, resigned July 21, 1865, surgeons certificate.
†Daniel D. Diffenbaugh.

1st LIEUTENANTS.

Thos. M. Hood, died at Shiloh of wounds received at Shiloh, April 6, 1862.
Moses R. Thompson, died at Bolivar, Tenn., October 10, 1862 of wounds received at the Hatchee, October 5, 1862.
Robert Smith, promoted to Captain June 16, 1863.
Thomas Allen, resigned August 11, 1863.
Michael J. Cooper, resigned July 12, 1864.
Samuel Buchanan, promoted to Captain March 20, 1865.
Daniel D. Diffenbaugh, promoted to Captain October 1, 1865.
†Thomas C. Laird.

2nd LIEUTENANTS.

Moses R. Thompson, promoted to 1st Lieutenant, April 21, 1862.
Robert Smith, promoted to 1st Lieutenant, October 16, 1862.
Thomas Allen, promoted to 1st Lieutenant, June 16, 1863.

Michael J. Cooper, promoted to 1st Lieutenant. November 14, 1863.
Samuel Buchanan, promoted to 1st Lieutenant, August 23, 1864.
Daniel D. Diffenbaugh, promoted to 1st Lieutenant, March 20, 1865.
Thomas C. Laird, promoted to 1st Lieutenant, October 1, 1865.
†Thomas E. Joiner.

1st SERGEANTS.

Robert Smith, promoted to 2d Lieutenant, April 24, 1862.
Michael J. Cooper, promoted to 2d Lieutenant, June 16, 1863.
Samuel Buchanan, promoted to 2d Lieutenant, April 14, 1864.
Daniel D. Diffenbaugh, promoted to 2d Lieutenant, August 23, 1864.
Thomas C. Laird, promoted to 2d Lieutenant, April 9. 1865.
Thomas E. Joiner, promoted to 2d Lieutenant, October 1, 1865.
‡Rudolph Kencke, vet.

SERGEANTS.

Wm. Swansey, promoted to Sergeant Major, December 7, 1861.
Joseph M. McKibben, reduced to the ranks at his request, Dec. 15, 1861.
Joseph Stamp, died of disease June 10, 1862.
James B. Smith, discharged August 23, 1863.
Robert C. Young, discharged Nov. 12, 1861, reduced to ranks.
Michael J. Cooper, promoted to 1st Sergeant, July 1, 1862.
Samuel Buchanan, promoted to 1st Sergeant, June 30, 1863.
Daniel D. Diffenbaugh, promoted to 1st Sergeant, April 1, 1863.
Thomas C. Laird, promoted to 1st Sergeant, September 1, 1864.
†Seth Cable, vet.
Thomas E. Joiner, promoted to 1st Sergeant, April 10, 1865.
Aaron Fehr, reduced to ranks, January 7, 1865.
Rudolph Kencke, vet., appointed 1st Sergeant, October 1, 1865.
†Firdinand Loehle, vet.
James S. Chambers, reduced to ranks, 1865.
†David Allison, vet.
†Lewis B. Richmond, vet.

CORPORALS,

Samuel E. Hershey, transferred to invalid corps, November 10, 1863.
Joseph S. Brown, died April 28, 1862, of wounds received at Shiloh.
John W. Rowrey, discharged, June 21, 1862.
Thomas Snyder, discharged, December 11, 1862.
David W. Fiscus, Discharged. Dec. 24, 1862.
Reuben Brubaker, died May 8, 1862 of wounds received at Shiloh.
Lewis B. Richmond, vet., appointed Sergeant, October 1, 1865.
Sidney A. Ward, died July 8, 1863, of wounds received at Jackson, Miss.
Daniel D. Diffenbaugh, promoted to Sergeant, July 1, 1862.
Samuel Buchanan, promoted to Sergeant May 1, 1862.
Thomas C. Laird, promoted to Sergeant, July 1, 1862.
Seth Cable, promoted to Sergeant. July 1, 1862.
Aaron Fehr, promoted to Sergeant, May 1, 1864.
Thomas E. Joiner, promoted to Sergeant, May 1, 1864.
Jonathan McMurray, discharged, May 20, 1863.
Charles Spooner, reduced to ranks, October, 1863.
Wm. Helm. died of disease, June 22, 1863.
Elias D. Baker, reduced to ranks.
Rudolph Kencke, promoted to Sergeant, September 1, 1864.
Ferdinand Leohle, promoted to Sergeant, March 1, 1865.
Isaac S. Lee, reduced to ranks, May, 1864.
Chambers McMurray, prisoner of war from August 27, 1864.
James S. Chambers, promoted to Sergeant, April 6, 1865.
Edward H. Baker, mustered out, June 19, 1865, War Department order.
David Allison, promoted to Sergeant, June 1, 1865.
John Wilson, reduced to ranks, January, 1864.
✠Francis Redinger, deserted, October 29, 1865.
†Newton Linsley, vet.
†James H. Haughey.
‡Ezekiel S. Clark.
†Uriah Richards.
†Aaron Fehe, vet.

PRIVATES.

†Albright Jacob, vet.
Allison David, vet., promoted Corporal, June 1, 1864.
Auman John, discharged, March 22, 1865.
Allen Thomas, promoted 2d Lieutenant, October 16, 1863.
Aikey Robert, died April 9, 1862, of wounds received at Shiloh.
†Albright Wm.
‡Angle Luther.
†Aikey Abraham.
Buchanan Samuel, vet., promoted to Corporal, April 1, 1862.
Brubaker Reuben, promoted to Corporal, December 15, 1861.
Beler Geo. D., killed at Shiloh, April 6, 1862.
Brown Wm., discharged, June 30, 1862.
†Benton Geo., discharged, Dec. 22, 1862, re-enlisted as vet. Feb. 29. 1864.
Brown Joseph S., promoted to Corporal, October 15, 1861.
Bradshaw Benj. H., promoted to Assistant Surgeon, September 12, 1862.
‡Baker Elias D., vet., promoted to Corporal, July 1, 1862.

Bates Branan L., died of disease, July 12, 1862.
Bush Wm., discharged February 9, 1863.
Baker Edward H., promoted to Corporal June 1, 1864.
Baker Solomon S., discharged May 24, 1865.
†Brubaker Wm. H. H.
†Baker Joseph.
†Beedy Eldridge H.
†Barfoot Frank R.
†Bardner Henry.
†Brew Ferdinand.
†Belliman John.
†Boyer Owen.
Buttler Elijah M., mustered out Jan. 8, 1866, expiration of term; transferred from 99th Illinois.
†Baker John M.
Cupple Calvin J., died of disease Nov. 7, 1865; transferred from 99th Ill's
Cable Seth, promoted to Corporal May 1, 1862.
Cable David, discharged October 19, 1864,
Cole James, discharged August 18,1862.
Craig Edwin W., discharged June 21, 1862.
Cooper Michael J., promoted to Sergeant December 15, 1861.
Clubine Daniel, discharged June 30, 1863.
Curtis Henry H., discharged November 11, 1862.
Clark Ezekiel S., promoted to Corporal May 1, 1865.
Christman Frank, discharged May 22, 1865.
Cable Elmas, discharged June 19, 1865.
†Campbell Richard.
†Cable William.
Carrel Daniel, mustered out June 9, 1864.
†Cole John.
†Chambers James S., promoted to Corporal April 11, 1864.
Diffenbaugh Daniel D., promoted to Corporal December 15, 1861.
Drake Edwin, discharged November 12, 1864, expiration of term.
Daughenbaugh Samuel, vet., dishonorably discharged Oct. 17, 1865.
Dunn Thomas, vet., deserted October 31, 1865.
Driesbach Daniel, died of disease March 12, 1863.
Daws Alfred, deserted November 2, 1865.
†Daws Thomas J.
Fehr Aaron, vet., promoted to Corporal June 1, 1862.
†Fiscus David W., re-enlisted February 28, 1864.
†Frisble Charles G.
Frisble Wm. D., deserted October 29, 1865.
Graken Samuel H., died April, 1862.
†Gage Isaac, vet.
†Gardner John.
†Groff John.
†Garman Henry C.
†Garman Wm. A.
†Goodrich Jerome.
Hulet Henry, died of disease May 30, 1862.
†Heekle Elias, vet.
Helm Wm., promoted Corporal July 1, 1862.
†Hood Joseph R., vet.
Hood Thomas J., deserted March 20,1864.
Hershey Samuel E., promoted Corporal October 15, 1861.
Hathaway Earl, re-enlisted in 2d Illinois Light Artillery Jan. 4, 1864.
Havard Wm., transferred to K Co. 46th Illinois Volunteers.
Haines Wm., died of disease, February 12, 1865.
†Haines John H.
Haughey James H., promoted Corporal April 10, 1865.
†Haughey Samuel J.
Hay Johathan, discharged March 30, 1865.
Hall Thomas W., mustered out October 3, 1865, expiration of term.
†Hathaway Robert.
†Johnston Wm. H.
Joiner Thomas E., promoted to Corporal June 1, 1862.
Jahn Francisco B., discharged by sentance of court martial Jan. 22, 1866.
Klantz Geo., vet., prisoner of war from August 27, 1864.
Keneke Rudolph, vet., promoted to Corporal July 1, 1862.
Kettner George, died April 12, 1862, of wounds received at Shiloh.
Krumme Henry, discharged Sept. 13, 1864, transferred from C company.
Klontz Peter, discharged May 5, 1865.
Laird Thomas C., vet., promoted Corporal May 1, 1862.
†Lee Ion, vet.
†Lee Isaac S., vet., promoted Corporal March 16, 1863.
Linsley Newton, vet., promoted Corporal March 1, 1865.
Long Casper, discharged July 9, 1862.
LeBell Peter, died of disease June 2, 1862.
Larrie John, died of disease June 27, 1863.
Lahay James, transferred to company K, 40th Illinois.
Leohle Ferdinand, vet., promoted to Corporal March 15, 1863.
†Lowe Thomas A.
†Law Rolandus.

†Lapp Joseph.
Moothart Pheau, discharged May 9, 1862.
Moothart John F., died of disease February 9, 1864.
†Motter Jonathan, vet.
Meinhart Conrad, discharged November 12, 1864.
†McMurray Jonathan, promoted Corporal July 1, 1862.
McMurray Chambers, vet., promoted Corporal April 11, 1864.
McKibben Joseph M., transferred to company K, 46th Illinois.
McLaughlin Thomas, transferred to company K, 46th Illinois.
McClintic John N., discharged March 17, 1863.
†McMurray George.
†Mayer Isaac.
†McLeas Robert.
Pricing George, killed in battle at Jackson, Miss., July 6, 1864.
†Petrick Paul, vet.
†Paul William.
†Pease Yeedock, transferred from 99th Illinois Infantry.
†Riddle William,   "   "   "   "
Richmond Lewis B., vet., promoted Corporal December 15, 1861.
Richard Uriah, promoted Corporal July 1, 1864.
Richard Wm. D., discharged October 13, 1864.
Rubold Henry, discharged March 8, 1865.
Reeter Wm., discharged November 12, 1864.
Rowry John W., promoted Corporal October 15, 1861.
Redinger Francis, vet., promoted Corporal February 1, 1865.
Rutter Jacob, deserted April 20, 1862.
Reasinyer Henry, died July 20, 1864, of wounds received at the battle of Jackson Miss.
Realt Edward, discharged August 9, 1865.
†Rutter Benj. F,
Rishel Elias, discharged August 9. 1865.
†Riddle Samuel.
†Raymen John A.
†Raymen Wm. H.
Smith Augustus L., discharged December 11, 1862.
†Smith Wm., vet.
Smith James B., promoted Sergeant October 15, 1861.
Smith Robert, promoted 1st Sergeant October 15, 1861.
Stamp Joseph, promoted Sergeant October 15, 1861.
Swanzey Wm., promoted Sergeant October 15, 1861.
†Sindlinger Wm. M., discharged July 9, 1863, re-enlisted July 28, 1865.
Shively John, died April 23, 1862, of wounds received at Shiloh.
Schrubb Thomas, discharged November 25, 1862.
Snyder Thomas, promoted Corporal, October 15, 1861.
Smith Martin, vet., died of disease March 24, 1864.
Steele James W., promoted Hospital Steward September 20, 1862.
Shaffer Jacob, died of disease July 17, 1862.
†Spooner Charles, vet., promoted Corporal July 1, 1862.
Shirk Daniel F., vet., deserted June 4, 1864.
Stamm Wm. D., died of disease September 24, 1864.
†Smith Edward O. W.
Shinkle John T., died of disease August 28, 1864.
Shippey Joseph W., died of Disease November 23, 1864.
Shearer John, died of disease, December 26, 1864.
†Sausman John S.
†Springman Adam.
Stamm Amos A., mustered out October 1865—expiration term of service.
†Sindlinger Samuel.
†Seeley Orrin.
†Sherman Leonard, transferred from company A.
†Scott Lorenzo D., transferred from 99th Illinois Infantry.
Tombleson Silas W., mustered out October 1865—expiration of term.
Tool Albert S., mustered out October 1865—expiration of term.
Tool Eugene T., mustered out October 1865—expiration of term.
†Thomas Wm. H.
†Vore John, vet.
Williams Peter, vet., died of disease March 3, 1865.
†Wilson Francis T., vet.
†Wilson John, vet., promoted Corporal September 1, 1864.
Wyer John, discharged April 26, 1863.
Ward Sidney A., vet., promoted Corporal December 25, 1861.
†Wentz, Philip, vet.
Weaver Wm., discharged December 5, 1864.
Wike Peter, transferred to Invalid corps November 10, 1863.
Wooten James E., deserted October 21, 1865.
Williams Wm., died of disease December 14, 1864.
†Walters Samuel.
Wolfinger Aaron, died of disease June 19, 1865.
†Wells Henry, transferred from 99th Illinois.
†Young David D.
Young Francis M., discharged October 19, 1864.
Young Robert C., promoted to Sergeant Dec. 15, 1863, mustered out Oct., 1864—expiration of term.

COMPANY "H."

CAPTAINS.
John Stevens, killed April 6, 1862, at the battle of Shiloh.
John A. Hughes, mustered out Dec. 6, 1864—expiration of term.
†Fred W. Pike.

1st LIEUTENANTS.
John A. Hughes, promoted Captain April 6, 1862.
Fred. W. Pike, promoted Captain December 6, 1864.
†Thomas A. Peironnet.

2d LIEUTENANTS.
Fred. W. Pike, promoted 1st Lieutenant April 6, 1862.
Edward A. Snyder, mustered out December 16, 1864.
†William P. Hardy.

1st SERGEANTS.
Thomas A. Peironnet, promoted 1st Lieutenant December 1, 1864.
Wm. P. Hardy, promoted 2d Lieutenant September 1, 1865.
†James Dorman.

SERGEANTS.
William P. Hardy, appointed 1st Sergeant April 9, 1865.
John M. Murphy, reduced to ranks November 2, 1862.
Charles C. Mason, killed at Shiloh April 6, 1862.
Ebenezer McCoulugh, discharged April 4, 1862.
Devillia D. Segnor, discharged October 4, 1862.
David Chapman, mustered out December 5, 1865—expiration of term.
John Meighan, reduced to the ranks November 2, 1862.
James Dorman, appointed 1st Sergeant September 1, 1865.
Wm. N. Henrie, reduced to the ranks.
John P. McGrath, transferred to veteran reserve corps.
Wm. M. Patterson, deserted November 19, 1865.
†James Patterson.
†Edward H. Reynolds.
†Corydon Stone.

CORPORALS.
E. H. Blackburn, discharged October 19, 1862.
DeWitt C. Bennett, reduced to ranks at his request.
A. J. Cooley, deserted January 28, 1863.
Wm. McDonald, reduced to the ranks.
Abram Fuller, discharged July 27, 1862.
Samuel D. Hemenway, reduced to the ranks at his request May 1, 1864.
Wm. P. Hardy, appointed Sergeant October 1, 1862.
Wm. H. Cook, mustered out December 1, 1864.
James Dorman, appointed Sergeant December 6, 1862.
Preston K. Hill, mustered out December 5, 1864.
James Patterson, appointed Sergeant December 5, 1864.
John Ure, mustered out November 21, 1864.
Henry McCarl, died of disease February 16, 1864.
Michael Rooch, reduced to ranks April 17, 1864.
Edward H. Reynolds, appointed Sergeant February 1, 1865.
Corydon Stone, appointed Sergeant April 9, 1865.
Charles Keniston, reduced to ranks November 17, 1865.
John P. McGrath, appointed Sergeant December 6, 1863.
Wm. M. Patterson, appointed Sergeant September 1, 1865.
John Meighan, died of disease December 19, 1865.
George W. Williams, deserted November 17, 1865.
James Landy, died at home, 1865.
James K. Seehler, reduced to ranks at his own request Feb. 1, 1865.
John Gorman, appointed Sergeant November 17, 1865.
†Charles B. Hardy.
James B. Newbery, appointed Sergeant December 1, 1865.
†Cornelius Kallager.
†Alva D. Akins.
†Kinney Wood.
†Woodbury Akins.
†Jacob Wood.
†Henry R. Ojers.

PRIVATES.
Antisdel Moses, discharged April 4, 1862.
Atkins Alva D., appointed Corporal November 17, 1865.
Atkins Woodbury, appointed Corporal November 17, 1865.
†Antenham Herman.
Adams Anderson, mustered out May 13, 1865.
Bond John, deserted April 7, 1862.
Bullis Abram F., discharged September 23, 1862.
Bullock Charles, deserted January 4, 1862.
Blaker Geo. M., deserted July 16, 1862.
†Bennet DeWitt C, vet.
Blackman F. H. appointed Corporal.

†Bennett Edward.
†Bailey Emery D.
†Bailey Albert.
Buttz Christian M., transferred from 99th Ill. Infantry, mustered out Jan. 11, 1866—expiration of term.
†Brown Joseph, transferred from 11th Illinois Infantry.
Baldwin Lewis E. transferred from 11th Ill. Infantry, mustered out Oct., 1865—expiration of term.
Burroughs Wm. H., transferred from 11th Ill. Infantry, mustered out Oct. 1865—expiration of term.
†Brace Sylvester N., transferred from 11th Illinois Infantry.
Cooley Anderson J., deserted January 28, 1863.
Cook Wm. H., appointed Corporal December 1, 1861.
†Cook Lyman H., vet.
†Cook Monroe, vet.
Chapman David, appointed Sergeant April 6, 1862.
†Cosort Samuel F., vet.
Carpenter Wm. I., discharged October 16, 1862.
Carpenter Denning, transferred to veteran reserve corps Nov. 11, 1863.
Coyle John, died May 8, 1863, of disease.
Ceames Frederick, transferred to company C, December 26, 1863.
Case Franklin, transferred to company D December 1, 1861.
Clank Jacob T., transferred to 23d Illinois Volunteers January 1, 1862.
†Case E. B.
Chambers Geo. W., died of disease January 26, 1863.
Corbin O. A., deserted October 31, 1865.
Commisky Thomas, mustered out May 2, 1865,
†Cosgrove Michael, transferred from company I July 1, 1864.
Carmichael John, mustered out October 31, 1865—expiration of term.
†Cohen Aaron, transferred from 99th Illinois Infantry.
Chase Everett E. transferred from 11th Ill. Infantry, mustered out Oct. 8, 1865—expiration of term.
Campbell Joseph A., transferred from 11th Ill. Infantry, died Aug. 18, 1865.
†Collins Dennis, transferred from 11th Illinois Infantry.
Dwyer Wm., transferred to veteran reserve corps Nov. 11, 1863.
Dolan James I., discharged Jan· 10, 1864, to accept promotion in the 6th U. S. C. A.
Dorman James, vet., appointed Sergeant December 6, 1862.
Dailey Patrick, died April 6, 1862, of wounds received at Shiloh.
Dunn James, discharged September 20, 1862.
†Dumphey Wm., vet.
Dunn Patrick, mustered out August 14, 1865—expiration of term.
†Doninger Addison.
DeWitt Ralph, transferred from 11th Illinois Infantry—mustered out Oct. 11, 1865—expiration of term.
Emerson Jerome, died Feb. 16, 1862, of wounds received at Ft. Donelson.
†Earnest Jacob, transferred from 11th Illinois Infantry.
Foy Peter, died April 4, 1862.
Fitzgerald John, vet., died January 7, 1865.
Fuller Abram, appointed Corporal December 1, 1861.
Fox Ferdinand, discharged November 25, 1862.
Green Phileman, drowned October 8, 1862.
Gonnan John, vet., appointed Corporal April 9, 1865.
Horton Burton M., discharged February 4, 1863.
Hughes John A., promoted to 1st Lieutenant December 1, 1861.
Horton Sylvester, died May 18, 1862.
†Horton Nelson J., vet.
Hill Preston K., appointed Corporal November 20, 1862.
†Hardy Robert, vet.
Hardy Wm. P., vet., appointed Corporal December 1, 1861.
Henric Wm. N., appointed Sergeant December 1, 1863—discharged December 5, 1863.
†Hemenway Samuel D., vet.
Hardy Charles B., appointed Corporal February 5, 1865.
Herrick O. B., mustered out May 4, 1865.
†Huntley Livingston.
†Horton Benjamin.
†Hochstoetter Wm.
†Horton Myron D.
†Hileman Thomas, transferred from 11th Illinois Infantry.
†Hileman John H., transferred from 11th Illinois Infantry.
Holmes James A., transferred from 11th Ill. Infantry—mustered out Oct. 1865—expiration of term.
Hicks Willard I., transferred from 11th Ill. Infantry—mustered out Oct. 1865—expiration of term.
Jones John J., appointed Lieut. Col. December 31, 1861.
Kenaston Charles H., vet., appointed Corporal December 6, 1863.
†Kiersey Geo. W., vet.
Kleman John, discharged for disability July 17, 1865.
†Kelley John W.
Kalaher Cornelius, appointed Corporal June 1, 1865.
†King Andrew.
†Keller James M., transferred from 11th Illinois Infantry.

Larson Andrew, discharged December 22, 1862.
†Little Isaac, vet.
Loveridge Jerome, died July 30, 1864.
Landy James, appointed Corporal December 5. 1864.
Lawless John, transferred from 11th Ill. Infantry—mustered out Oct. 18 1865—expiration of term.
McCarl Henry, appointed Corporal October 1, 1861.
McGrath John P., vet., appointed Corporal October 1, 1862.
McConlaugh E., appointed Sergeant October 14, 1861.
McDowell David, mustered out December 5, 1864.
Meighan John, vet., appointed Corporal December 6, 1863.
Murphy John M., discharged November 2, 1864,
Mason Charles C., appointed Sergeant October 1, 1861.
McSweeney Wm.. died December 1, 1865.
McDonald Wm., appointed Corporal November 5, 1862, deserted 1863.
Miller Henry C., transferred to veteran reserve corps Nov. 16, 1883.
Merchant Myron V., discharged April 4, 1862.
†Murphy Murtha.
†Martin Don V.
†Meighan Thomas.
McBride Thomas, died July 18, 1865,
Moore Henry, mustered out May 1865, A G O No 77.
†Millard Morey.
†Miller Sanford.
†Mayer Michael.
Morgon Geo. F., transferred from 11th Illinois Infantry—mustered out October 1865—expiration of term.
Muddoon Barney, transferred from 11th Illinois Infantry—mustered out October 1865—expiration of term.
Newberry Jas. B., vet., appointed Corporal April 9, 1865.
Nugent Patrick, transferred from compauy I—taansferred to veteran reserve corps November 11, 1863.
†Neer Barton B.
Ojers Henry R., appointed Corporal December 1, 1865.
Pike Fred W., apointed 2d Lieutenant December 1, 1861.
Perry Geo. H., discharged November 1862.
Patterson Wm. N., vet., appointed Corporal December 6, 1863.
Patterson Alexander, deserted April 30, 1862.
Parker Shepherd P., deserted August 1, 1862.
Peironnet Thomas A., vet., appointed 1st Sergeant October 1, 1861.
Pettis George dropped at special muster August 18, 1862.
†Pethrof John.
Page Scott, deserted Jan 1864.
Powers Martin, discharged August 18, 1865.
†Patterson Rease G.
Pells Simon P., mustered out Aug, 1865—expiration of term.
†Peironnet John A., transferred from 11th Illinois Infantry, vel.
Quick Joseph W. V., died May 1, 1862 of wounds at Shiloh.
Reynolds Edward H., vet., appointed Corporal Dec 6, 1863.
†Roach Michael, vet., appointed Corporal December 12. 1863.
†Ready Peter, mustered out Dec. 5, 1864—expiration of term—re-enlisted January 20, 1865.
Robertson Charles F., died June 20, 1864.
Reynolds Walter S., mustered out May 22, 1865—expiration of term.
†Reach Martin.
Stevens John, appointed Captain December 1, 1861.
Smith Zerah O., discharged April 4, 1862.
Segnor Devilla D., appointed Sergeant November 6, 1861.
Schronmaker Andrew, discharged June 16, 1862.
Snyder John E. died May 1, 1862.
Sperry Justice, deserted January 4. 1862.
Smith John, discharged April 4, 1862.
Stone Chas. H., discharged July 20, 1862.
Stone Corydon, vet., appointed Corporal May 1, 1864.
†Smith John.
Sechler James M., appointed Corporal April 1, 1864.
†Saunders Geo. H.
Sullivan Michael, mustered out October 10—expiration of term.
Sullivan Garnett, mustered out October 10—expiration of term.
Snyder E. A., appointed 2d Lieutenant September 1, 1862.
†Sells Eliend. transferred from 99th Illinois Infantry.
Sausman John B., transferred from 11th Illinois Infantry—mustered out October 1865—expiration of term.
Townsend Luther, died at Mt. Vernon, Indiana.
†Talley William, vet.
Tracy James, discharged October 18, 1862.
Tracy Stanton C., discharged June 16, 1862.
†Throop Freeman W.
†Tilcher John.
Thrasher Wm., transferred from 11th Illinois—mustered out Oct. 1865—expiration of term.
Ure John, appointed Corporal July 1, 1862.
†Wertz Upton, vet.

Welsh Theron, deserted May 7, 1862.
Whalen James, vet., discharged July 21, 1865.
Wood Jacob, vet., appointed Corporal December 1, 1865.
Wear George W., discharged August 19, 1863.
Williams George W., appointed Corporal December 5, 1864.
Williams Stephen E., transferred to veteran reserve corps Nov. 11, 1863.
Wood Kenney, appointed Corporal November 1865.
†Way Chas. R.
†Wood George H.
†Wicks Charles H.
Wiles Jepthath A., transferred from 11th Ill. Infantry—mustered out Nov. 27, 1865—expiration of term.
Wiley Henry E., transferred from 11th Ill. Infantry—mustered out Oct. 8, 1865—expiration of term.

COMPANY "I."

CAPTAINS.

Charles P. Stinson, resigned Feb. 16, 1862
Rosiel D. Campbell, resigned Aug. 31, 1862.
†David S. Pride.

1st LIEUTENANTS.

James Ballard, resigned Nov. 19, 1862.
†Hezekiah Bullock.

2d LIEUTENANTS.

Wm. H. Howell, killed at Shiloh, April 6, 1862.
Hezekiah Bullock, promoted 1st Lieut. March 13, 1863.
Uriah J. Terry,* mustered out expiration of term, Nov. 30, 1864.
†Henry G. Kennelley.

1st SERGEANTS.

Hezekiah Bullock, promoted to 2d Lieut. June 26, 1862.
John St. John, discharged Nov. 19, 1862.
Henry G. Kennelley, promoted 2d Lieut. Aug. 4, 1865.
†Solomon A. Shiffer.

SERGEANTS.

John St. John, appointed 1st Sergeant June 26, 1862.
Harvey P. Sargent, reduced to ranks March 31, 1862.
Charles L. Pratt, transferred to 2d Ills. Lt. Art. June 1, 1862.
Henry G. Kennelley, appointed 1st Sergeant May 18, 1863.
John Collins, killed at Shiloh April 6, 1862.
Solomon A. Shiffer, appointed 1st Sergeant Sept. 1, 1865.
James W. Holmes,* discharged May 25, 1863.
Jacob P. Miller* discharged Sept. 21, 1863.
Lewis Manchester,* mustered out Nov. 30, 1864—expiration of term.
Jacob Post,* reduced to ranks, May 15, 1865, at his own request.
†Lorenzo Kipley,* vet.
†George W. Relman.
†Philander Woolsey,* vet.
†Mather H. Trask, transferred from 11th Ills. Infantry.

CORPORALS.

Russell D. Carter, died April 5, 1862.
David B. Rossiter, died May 27, 1865.
Wm. H. Robbins, died April, 1862.
Judson Ware, deserted July 4, 1862.
James H. Davis, appointed Q. M. Sergeant.
Van R. Strong, reduced to ranks, Nov. 2, 1863.
Lewis Shiffer, reduced to ranks.
Cyrus Booth, transferred to invalid corps, March 2, 1864.
Solomon A. Shiffer, appointed Sergeant May 1, 1863.
Jerome R. Holton,* reduced to ranks Feb. 3, 1865.
Jacob A. Post,* appointed Sergeant Nov. 2, 1863.
James F. Beebe, reduced to ranks Feb. 3, 1865.
†Emanuel F. Brown.
Charles L. Beebe,* reduced to ranks Feb. 1, 1865.
†Eugene Parmln.
†George P. Shipman.
†John A. Morris,* vet.
Philander H. Woolsey,* vet., appointed Sergeant Sept. 1, 1865.
†Benjamin W. Morse,* vet.
†Almon W. Bennett, vet., reduced to ranks, Nov., 1865,
Joel P. Keyes,* discharged to accept promotion in colored organization, May, 1863.

PRIVATES.

†Abbott Jacob B., vet.
Alford Harry, died of disease, April, 1862.
Aster Frank, killed at Shiloh, April 6, 1862.
Averill George, discharged, 1862.
Anderson George, deserted Aug. 18, 1865.
†Arnold Abraham.
†Bennett Almon W. vet.
Boyd Nelson, discharged Dec. 29, 1862.
Bates John, died of disease Nov. 18, 1862.
Booth Henry, transferred to invalid corps April 2, 1864.
Brown Emanuel F., vet., appointed Corporal Nov, 1, 1863.
†Brown Franklin S., vet.
Barron Henry, discharged July 9, 1862.
Burns Michael R., mustered out Nov. 30, 1864.
Burns Mitchell, deserted Jan. 1, 1862.
†Beebe James F., appointed Corporal Nov., 1863.
Bennett Charles F., appointed Hospital Steward U. S. A.
Barnard Geo. S.,*mustered out Nov. 30, 1864.
†Benjamin Porter,* vet.
Briscoe Edward, transferred from 99th Ills. Inf., mustered out Oct. 8, 1865—expiration of term.
†Benjamin George.
†Chasm Thomas.
Curtis Wm., discharged Oct. 18, 1862.
Cooper George H., died of disease June 19, 1862.
Cole Cornelius C., died of disease Nov. 4, 1864.
Cummings Ezra J., discharged April 3, 1862.
Campbell Rosiel D., promoted Captain Feb. 26, 1862.
†Corkins Wallace.
Campbell Charles R., discharged Aug.,'1862.
Campbell Wm. L., died of disease, May 19, 1862.
Cannon Curtis, transferred to invalid corps, March 2, 1864.
Clark Rothchild N., died of disease, June 22, 1862.
Corsort John, died of disease, Jan. 2, 1864.
Cosgrove Patrick, transferred to invalid corps, April 2, 1864.
Cromwell Daniel,* vet., killed at battle Jackson Miss., July 7, 1864.
Crawford Samuel E.,* died of disease March, 1863.
†Clay Charles H., transferred from 11th Ills. Inf.
†Cure Wm. M., transferred from 11th Ills. Inf.
Cowen John R., transferred from 11th Ills. Inft.—mustered out Oct. 1865—expiration of term.
Claypool Elisha, transferred from 11th Ills. Inf.—mustered out Oct. 1865—expiration of term.
Cosgrove Michael, transferred to H Co., July 1. 1864.
†Courier Lorenzo.
†Cleaveland John K.
†Colton Orim.
Dow John W.,* vet., killed near Jackson, Miss., July 7, 1864.
Donnovan Dennis,* mustered out Nov. 30, 1864—expiration of term.
†Davenport George A., transferred from 11th Illinois Infantry
Dilion Henry, transferred from 99th Illinois Infantry—mustered out Dec. 1, 1865—expiration of term.
†Davis James H., appointed Corporal December 1, 1861.
‡Davis Wm. H., transferred from 118th Illinois Mounted Infantry.
Echelbarger Benj. F., * transferred to invalid corps Jan. 5, 1864.
†Fox Fredinand W.
†Forbes Hardan P.,* vet.
Fisher Wilson J., transferred from 11th Illinois Infantry—mustered out October 8, 1865—expiration of term.
Fowler John, transferred from 11th Illinois Infantry—mustered out October 8, 1865—expiration of term.
Frey James, transferred from 11th Illinois Infantry—mustered out October 8, 1865—expiration of term.
Fisher Thomas B., transferred from 11th Illinois Infantry—mustered out October 8, 1865—expiration of term.
†Gailer Willet P., vet.
Goss Alonzo, mustered out November 30, 1864—expiration of term.
Graves Aspasia, * mustered out November 30, 1864—expiration of term.
Gardinier Chas. H., transferred from 11th Illinois Infantry—mustered out October 8, 1865—expiration of term.
†Guill Jefferson.
†Hormell Lewis C.
†Hormell Cornelius H.
Hills Joseph, died of disease June 10, 1862.
†Hobday James.
Hight John R., discharged November 25, 1862.
Helning Adam, discharged August 15, 1862.
Harris George, died of disease June 8, 1862.
Harman James E.,* mustered out Nov. 30, 1864—expiration of term.
†Howard Frank,* vet.
†Holton Jerome R.,* vet.

Harris Alanson C., transferred from 11th Illinois Infantry—mustered out October 8, 1865—expiration of term.
Harris Wm. A., transferred from 11th Illinois Infantry—mustered out Oct. 8, 1865—expiration of term.
†Horseman Charles F., transferred from 11th Illinois Infantry.
Hunter John D., transferred from 11th Ill. Infantry—mustered out Oct. 3, 1865—expiration of term.
Hunter Morrison, transferred from 11th Ill. Infantry—mustered out Oct. 3, 1865—expiration of term.
Hutson Alfred, transferred from 11th Ill. Infantry—discharged Sep. 1865.
Huber George, transferred from 11th Ill. Infantry—mustered out October 12, 1865—expiration of term.
†Hill Hiram.
‡Johnson Albert S., vet., transferred from 11th Illinois Infantry.
‡Jackson Wm. A., transferred from 11th Illinois Infantry.
Kennelly Henry G., vet., appointed Sergeant May 1. 1862.
Kennelly Maurice, died of disease May 15, 1862.
Keightlinger Alexander, vet., deserted July 1, 1865.
Kent John R., deserted 1862.
Kent Marcellus B., mustered out Jan. 1, 1865—expiration of term.
†Kipley Lorenzo,* vet., appointed Sergeant March 22, 1864.
Keightlinger Carson, transferred from 11th Ill. Infantry—mustered out October 8, 1865—expiration of term.
‡Kimmel Geo., transferred from the 11th Illinois Infantry.
Keyes Joel P.,* appointed Corporal March 2, 1863.
‡Lucraft Joseph.
Lawton James E., mustered out Nov. 30, 1864—expiration of term.
Lawrence Milo, discharged November 25, 1862.
Larison Erie, mustered out Nov. 30, 1864—expiration of term.
‡Lasher George,* vet.
Larish Almon S.,* mustered out Nov. 30, 1864—expiration of term.
Leasch August, transferred from 11th Illinois Infantry—mustered out October 8, 1865—expiration of term.
‡Lorch Alexander, transferred from 11th Illinois Infantry.
‡Lee Daniel E.
McLaren Charles, vet., died of disease January 4, 1865.
Moray Henry C., discharged December 18, 1862.
Marcy Frank P., killed at Shiloh April 6, 1862.
Madden John, transferred to Invalid corps.
Marcy Andrew M., deserted August 18, 1862.
Madden John,* vet., died of disease at Amboy, Illinois.
‡Mellgan Jacob W.,* vet.
Morris John A.,* vet., appointed Corporal.
Morris David,* mustered out Nov. 30, 1864—expiration of term.
Morse Benj. W.,* appointed Corporal.
Myers James,* mustered out Nov. 30, 1864—expiration of term.
Munger Riley D, transferred from 11th Illinois Infantry—mustered out October 8, 1865—expiration of term.
Manuel Frank, transferred from 11th Ill. Infantry—mustered out October 8, 1865—expiration of term.
Morse Wm. E., transferred from 11th Ill. Infantry—mustered out October 8, 1865—expiration of term.
Merigold Arthur, transferred from 11th Ill. Infantry—mustered out October 8, 1865—expiration of term.
‡McCain Milford.
‡Mills Isaac, transferred from 118th Illinois Infantry.
Norris Wm. H. H., killed at Shiloh April 6, 1862.
Nugent Patrick, transferred to company H October 1, 1862.
‡Nunn Robert,* vet.
Nevors Alonzo, transferred from 11th Illinois Infantry—mustered out October 8, 1865—expiration of term.
North Charles H., died of disease November 3, 1864.
‡Osborne Thomas B.
Olney Ransom, discharged May 27, 1862.
O'Harra Thomas B., promoted 2d Lieutenant 56th Ill. Infantry 1865.
‡Post Jacob,* vet., appointed Sergeant July 1, 1864.
Pratt Herman, discharged May 20, 1862.
Pratt Newell, mustered out Nov. 30, 1864—expiration of term.
Pratt Charles L., appointed Sergeant December 1, 1861.
‡Parker Wm. N.
Parker Marion, mustered out Nov. 30, 1865—term expired.
Parker Elijah, deserted November 3, 1862.
‡Paul George, vet.
Parr David, discharged April 3, 1862.
Pinney Dwight, deserted January 1, 1862.
Price John W., deserted August 18, 1862.
‡Pugh John, vet., transferred from 11th Illinois Infantry.
Parmin Eugene, appointed Corporal May 15, 1865.
Root Samuel H., transferred to company E January 1, 1865.
Roff Clark P.,* mustered out November 30, 1864.
Ritz Martin L.,* mustered out November 30, 1864.
Relman Augustus C., died of disease August 31, 1865.
Relman George W., appointed Corporal.

Shiffer Solomon A., vet., appointed Corporal.
Shiffer Robert, deserted June 30, 1863.
‡Scott Jacob, vet.
Swanston Peter, transferred to company E April 1, 1863.
‡Stevens Elnathan, vet.
†Sarles Elijah.
Snyder Edward A., promoted to 2d Lieutenant company H.
†Sloan Ephraim, transferred from 11th Illinois Infantry.
Sheedy Patrick, transferred from 11th Illinois Infantry—mustered out October 8, 1865—expiration of term.
Shinkle John W., transferred from 99th Ill. Infantry—discharged May 24, 1865.
†Shipman Edgar W.
Shipman George P., appointed Corporal May 15, 1865.
†Snyder George W.
‡Sheedy James R.
Sawyer Horace P., died of disease September 1, 1865.
†Tearney Edward,* vet.
Thomas Eugene T.,* mustered out November 30—expiration of term.
†Thorne Jacob, transferred from 11th Illinois Infantry.
Ulm Robert R., transferred from 11th Ill. Infantry—mustered out October 12, 1865—expiration of term.
Vaughn Mathew, deserted September 5, 1862.
Vickey Chester, transferred from 11th Ill. Infantry—mustered out October 12, 1865—expiration of term.
‡Van Nedan Theodore, transferred from 11th Illinois Infantry.
West Alexander G., discharged August 16, 1862.
Wright Burgess, died of disease April 19, 1862.
Wing Horace J., discharged.
Wressell David,* mustered out November 30, 1864.
Whiting Henry B.,* transferred to invalid corps April 2, 1864.
‡Warren James, transferred from 11th Illinois Infantry.
‡Windland James, transferred from 11th Illinois Infantry.
‡Welty Tyras.
‡Winebrenner John B.,* vet.
Wier Thomas,* transferred to veteran reserve corps April 2, 1864.

* All names of men marked with an asterisk (*), were transferred from Company D., first organization, March 2d, 1863, by Special Order No. 8, A. G. O., State of Illinois.

COMPANY "K."

CAPTAINS.

John M. McCracken, promoted Major Jan. 13, 1863.
William Stewart, mustered out Dec. 21, 1864—term of service expired.
†Oley F. Johnson.

1st LIEUTENANTS.

William Stewart, promoted Captain Jan. 13, 1863.
Joseph McKibben, mustered out Dec. 15, 1864—term of service expired.
Lewis C. Butler, died of disease Oct. 5, 1865, at Salubrity Springs, La.
†John Wilson.

2d LIEUTENANTS.

Beverly W. Whitney, resigned July 16, 1862.
Joseph M. McKibben, promoted 1st Lieut. Jan. 13, 1863.
Oley F. Johnson, promoted Capt. May 4, 1865.
John Wilson, promoted 1st Lieut, Nov. 25, 1865.
†Thom James.

1st SERGEANTS.

James C. Mallory, reduced to ranks, Jan. 1, 1862.
Joseph M. McKibben, promoted to 2d Lieut., Aug. 16, 1862.
Oley F. Johnson, promoted to 2d Lieut., Jan. 13, 1863.
Lewis C. Butler, promoted to 1st Lieut., March 20, 1865.
Samuel D. Lamb, reduced to ranks, Dec. 11, 1865.
†Wm. Keeling.

SERGEANTS.

Lewis C. Butler, appointed 1st Sergeant, Jan. 13, 1863.
Oscar H. Osborne, discharged July 27, 1862.
Oley F. Johnson, appointed 1st Sergeant, Aug. 16, 1862.
George Barton, discharged Nov. 21, 1863.
Wilson John, promoted 2d Lieut, May 4, 1865.
James Thom, appointed 2d Lieut., Nov. 25, 1865.
John Hiath, discharged Feb. 11, 1863.

James H. Reed, discharged Aug. 31, 1863, to receive promotion in colored organization.
Richard N. Needham, reduced to ranks, June 7, 1864.
Samuel D. Lamb, promoted to 1st Sergeant, March 20, 1865.
†Oley Oleson.
Saul H. Kamorar, reduced to ranks, Dec. 11, 1865.
William Keeling, promoted 1st Sergeant, Dec. 12, 1865.
†Amandson John.
†Schele Anthony.

CORPORALS.

Walter G. Barnes. discharged May 31, 1862.
John Wilson, appointed Sergeant, Aug. 16, 1862.
Benj. R. Frisbie, reduced to ranks, Jan. 1, 1862. at his own request.
Timothy S. Felton, died of disease, March 17, 1862.
Reuben C. Hardy, discharged Sept. 7, 1863.
Elijah H. Gardner, died of disease. June 1, 1862.
James Thom, appointed Sergeant Dec. 30, 1862.
Thomas Woolcock, appointed Hospital Steward, April 1, 1864.
Samuel D. Lamb, appointed Sergeant, March 1, 1864.
Abijah L. F. M. Snow, discharged Aug. 29. 1862.
John Hiatt, appointed Sergeant, Aug. 16, 1862.
Oley Oleson, appointed Sergeant, June 7, 1864.
James H. Reed, appointed Sergeant, Feb. 11, 1863.
Saul H. Kamrar, appointed Sergeant, March 20, 1865.
William J. Eshelman, discharged Jan. 14, 1864.
Richard N. Needham, appointed Sergeant, July 4, 1863.
John Amandson, appointed Sergeant, Dec. 31, 1865.
William Keeling, appointed Sergeant, May 4, 1865.
Nathaniel Gitchell, discharged July 12, 1865.
Thomas Wood, reduced to ranks at his own request, Jan. 16, 1865.
Isaac Woodruff, reduced to ranks at his own request, Jan. 16, 1865.
Anthony Schele, appointed Sergeant, Dec. 31, 1865.
David Warner, reduced to ranks Nov. 30, 1865.
†Barton Mishler.
†John H. Miller.
†Wm. N. Wagner.
†Wm. Hartman.
†George N. Scott.
†Wm. Quinn.
‡Albert Zweifel.
†James McGurk.

PRIVATES.

Amandson John, vet., appointed Corporal Dec. 20, 1863.
Allen Thomas J., appointed Hospital Steward, Feb. 1, 1865.
†Artley Abram.
Apker John, died of disease, May 8, 1865.
†Artley Charles.
Butler James A., died of disease, July 13, 1862.
Butler Lewis C., vet., appointed Sergeant Nov. 7, 1861.
Byrne John A., discharged Aug. 11, 1865.
Burns Mose, discharged May 25, 1862.
Brown George H., died of disease, May 18, 1862.
Birdsall John A., deserted Aug. 18, 1862.
Barton George, appointed Sergeant Nov. 7, 1861.
Barnes Walter G., appointed Corporal Nov. 7, 1861.
Brace John D., died May 22, 1862, of wounds received at Shiloh.
Burns John discharged June 16, 1862.
Boyle Laughey, transferred to V. R. Corps, Sept. 25, 1863.
Baker John, mustered out Oct. 5, 1865—expiration of term.
†Butterfield Charles W.
Barker Dudley A., died of disease, June 17, 1865.
†Babb Amos W.
†Bride George H.
†Canfield Gideon G., vet.
Curran John, transferred to V. R. C., Sept. 25, 1863.
Curry Samuel T., transferred to V. R. C., April 28, 1863.
Crampton Aaron, discharged Sept. 9, 1862.
Cook George, discharged April 6, 1863.
‡Cantrill Joel T., vet., transferred from B Co.
Cooledge Nelson, discharged Oct. 4, 1864, of wounds received July 7, 1864, at Jackson, Miss.
†Cauvil Colvin.
Cade Alfred, deserted, Oct. 29, 1865.
Carrol Patrick, deserted, March 2, 1864.
†Cossler Amond.
†Daughenbaugh Wm. J., vet.
Dodson Thos. H., died of disease, June 1, 1862.
†Deimer Josiah, vet.
Dillon Michael, transferred to C Co., March 1, 1862.
†Dillon George W.
†Dillon Zacariah.

‡Devore Espy.
Dolan John, deserted March 4, 1864.
Dodson Jacob, died of disease, Oct. 30, 1864.
Doan Joseph, died of disease, May 28, 1864.
‡Decker Zackariah.
†Dinsmore Wm., transferred from 11th Ills. Inf.
Eshleman Wm. J., appointed Corporal, Aug. 17, 1862.
Ely Marion, died Aug. 8, 1864.
Felton Timothy S., died March 17, 1862.
Farley Thomas, transferred from Co. C, to V. R. C., Nov. 10, 1863.
Frisbie Benj. R. discharged Dec. 29, 1864—expiration of term.
Fry Conrad, mustered out June 19, 1865—expiration of term.
‡Flood Bartholomew, transferred from 11th Ills. Inf.
Gardner Elijah M., died of disease, June 3, 1862.
†Gilman Andrew, vet.
Gitchell Nathaniel, appointed Corporal March 1, 1864.
‡Gibler Howard.
Gresley Willis C., discharged June 12, 1865.
†Gresley Uriah.
Gillespie Peter, vet., transferred from E Co.—discharged May 22, 1865.
‡Grigsby John W.
‡Grigsby Samuel.
†Garrison Israel T., transferred from 99th Ills. Inf.
Hand Barney, died of disease, Dec. 23, 1861.
Hiatt John, appointed Corporal Jan. 1, 1862.
Hartman Wm., vet., appointed Corporal May 31, 1865.
Hardy Reuben C., appointed Corporal Nov. 7, 1861.
‡Holverson Matthias, vet.
Humphrey David, discharged May 19, 1862.
Hills Enos P., deserted Aug. 18, 1862.
Howard Wm., deserted Aug. 18, 1862.
Hays Thomas J., transferred to vet. res. corps, Nov. 10, 1863.
Hartman Amon, discharged July 19, 1865.
‡Heiter Monroe.
†Hays John R., transferred from 11th Illinois Infantry.
‡Hughes Wm., transferred from 11th Illinois Infantry.
Johnson Oley F., appointed Sergeant Nov. 7, 1861.
Jefferson Lewis, died of disease, June 20, 1862.
Kettleson Oley, died of disease, Dec. 19, 1861.
Kostenbader Daniel, discharged Nov. 24, 1862.
†Kenney Daniel, vet.
Keeling, Wm., vet., appointed Corporal March 1, 1864.
†Kamrar Abram W., vet.
‡Kamrar Saul H., vet., appointed Corporal Dec. 20, 1863.
†Kraft Jacob.
†Kelley Zebeldee.
‡Kamrar David.
†Keck Henry S.
‡Lamb Samuel D., vet,, appointed Corporal Nov. 7, 1861.
Lahey James, vet., died of amputation of leg, Feb. 19, 1865.
Latour Charles, transferred to Co. C, Jan. 1, 1862.
Logan Wm. deserted March 4, 1864.
†Leibhart Henry.
†Lower Reuben.
†Lamb Samuel F.
Linscott Abraham, transferred from 11th Illinois Infantry—mustered out October, 1865—expiration of term.
†McGurk James, vet., appointed Corporal Aug. 28, 1865.
Mallory James C., appointed 1st Sergeant Nov. 7, 1861, transferred to F Co., January 1, 1862.
Myran Thomas, died of disease, July 12, 1862.
Martin Wm. H., deserted May 31, 1862.
Miller Aaron, died of disease, June 6, 1862.
McKimson John S., discharged Dec. 29, 1864—expiration of term.
McLaughlin Thomas, vet., deserted Nov. 2, 1865.
McKibben Joseph M., transferred from G Co., Jan. 1, 1862—appointed 1st Sergeant January 1, 1862.
Mishler Barton, appointed Corporal March 1, 1864.
†Mullen Dominic.
Miller John H., appointed Corporal March 1, 1865.
†McCoy Geo.
†Muffley Charles T.
†McKibben James H.
Miller Ambrose, discharged June 24, 1865.
Mallory DeWitt C., discharged May 23, 1865.
†Modie Thomas J., transferred from 99th Illinois Volunteers.
†Morton Jeremiah, transferred from 99th Illinois Volunteers.
Mather Abijah, vet., transferred to Co. B, Jan. 17, 1865.
‡Needham Richard N., vet., appointed Corporal Dec. 30, 1862.
Newton James H., transferred to E Co., Dec. 1, 1864.
†Nicholas Charles H.
†Osborne Oscar, II., vet., appointed Sergeant Nov. 7, 1861.
Oleson Oley, vet., appointed Corporal August 17, 1862.

Oleson John, deserted August 18, 1862.
†Owen Albert.
Phillips Smith, vet., dishonorably discharged, May 8, 1865—sentence General Court-Martial.
Phillips Jesse, deserted July 15, 1865.
Parmlee Silas, discharged Dec. 29, 1864—expiration of term.
Patten Lawrence, discharged March 7, 1862.
†Plotner Frank.
Quinn Wm., vet., appointed Corporal Dec. 31, 1865.
Reagle Jacob, died of disease, Oct. 26, 1862.
Reed James H., appointed Corporal August 17, 1862.
†Butler Wm. H. H., vet.
†Rudle Leonard, vet.
Reber Martin Van B., discharged January 4, 1864.
‡Reber Levi M., vet.
†Runner Ziba. T. F.
†Richards Wm. D.
†Richards Levi.
Senterben Benjamin, deserted August 18, 1862.
Slade Thomas, vet., appointed principal musician, Dec. 20, 1863.
Scheie Anthony vet., appointed Corporal March 1, 1865.
Schock Robert, discharged August 26, 1862.
Snow Abijah, L. F. M., discharged August 27, 1862, of wounds received at Shiloh.
Segen Theodore, discharged August 27, 1862.
†Starr Frederick, H.
‡Scott Isaac.
Scott George W., appointed Corporal Dec. 1, 1865.
Strong Frederick, H., deserted March 4, 1864.
Shearer Wilson, mustered out October 7, 1865—expiration of term.
‡Spowage Wm,
‡Sweeley Lewis Z.
‡Shane Matthias.
‡Shane John W.
‡Smith Charles.
‡Sloan Thomas.
‡Sheffy Levi W.
‡Sheffer Thomas. J.
‡Silkwood James, H., transferred from 99th Illinois Infantry.
‡Tisinger Robert R., transferred from 99th Illinois Infantry.
Thom James, vet., appointed Corporal Nov. 7, 1861.
Thompson Neils, died of disease, May 13, 1862.
‡Thomas Wm.
‡Train Leonard R.
Winnie Daniel, discharged Dec. 29, 1864—expiration of term.
Wagner Wm. N., vet., appointed Corporal May 31, 1865.
†Woodruff Isaac vet., appointed Corporal March 1, 1864.
‡Warner David J., vet., appointed Corporal March 1, 1865.
‡Wood Thomas, vet., appointed Corporal March 1, 1864.
Wardwell Wm. G., vet., deserted July 15, 1865.
Wilson John, vet., appointed Corporal Nov. 7, 1861.
Walbridge Thomas vet., drowned in White River Ark., Nov. 28, 1864.
†Woolcock Thomas, vet., appointed Corporal December 26, 1861.
Wertz Peter, discharged Jan. 4, 1864—expiration of term.
Withneck Peter, died of disease, May 17, 1862.
‡Warner Wm. W.
Watson Henry, deserted October 4, 1865.
Winnie Abram, died of disease, June 16, 1865.
‡Whyte James T., transferred from 99th Illinois Infantry.
‡Williams Andsen J., transferred from 99th Illinois Infantry.
‡Zeigler Miller, transferred from B Co., April 1, 1864.
‡Zweifel Albert, appointed Corporal December 31, 1865.

All Officers and Enlisted Men marked thus (††) were mustered out with the Regiment January 20, 1866, at Baton Rouge, La., and received their discharge and final pay, at Springfield, Illinois, February 2, 1866.

LIBRARY
UNIVERSITY OF ILLINOIS
URBANA

HISTORICAL MEMORANDA

OF THE

46TH ILLINOIS VETERAN
VOLUNTEER INFANTRY,

FROM ITS ORGANIZATION.

PART FIRST.

The 46th Regiment Illinois Infantry Volunteers, composed of Companies A, B, C. G and K, from Stephenson County, and F from Richland County, rendezvoused at Camp Butler, Illinois, and Companies D, I, H and E from Lee, Ogle and Whiteside counties, rendezvoused at Dixon, Illinois, was organized at Camp Butler, Illinois, on the 28th day of December, 1861, under the command of Col. JOHN A. DAVIS, of Stephenson county, who labored assiduously while the Regiment was in camps of instruction to bring it up to a high state of drill and discipline, with very satisfactory results.

On the 11th day of February, 1862, the Regiment left Camp Butler by rail, via. Decatur, Ill's., arriving at Cairo the morning of the 12th. and immediately embarked on the Steamer "Belle Memphis" with orders to proceed up the Cumberland River and report to Gen. GRANT, before Fort Donelson, Tenn. After a very pleasant trip in company with the largest and most magnificent fleet of steamers ever before seen on the Cumberland River, the regiment landed on the west bank of the same on the morning of the 14th of February, three miles below Fort Donelson. The men were supplied with forty rounds of ammunition each and disembarked. Having no teams, nothing but what the men could carry could be taken along. Everything else was stored upon the muddy bank and a guard of invalids placed over it. A weary march of six miles was made to reach the Head Quarters of Gen. GRANT, to whom Col. DAVIS reported on the afternoon of February 14th. The Regiment was assigned to Gen. LEW WALLACE'S command, but was not ordered to the front until the morning of the 15th of February. Having no tents and only a limited supply of blankets and rations, the men suffered greatly during the cold and snowy night. It was a very rough initiation into the soldier's life, and few indeed were the number who did not wish for a speedy termination of the war and the termination of their enlistment.

On the morning of the 15th the Regiment was assigned a position near the right of the line where the rebels had the day previous attempted to cut their way through and where it was apprehended they would make another attempt. The regiment, however, with the exception of changing position several times during the day, rested quietly upon its arms until about three P. M., when it was ordered to the front and right to support a battery that was about to open on the enemy in their works. No sooner had the Regiment taken its position partially protected from the enemy's fire by a low ridge upon which the battery was posted, than the enemy opened a most terrific fire to dislodge our battery, which was annoying them very much, wounding three of our men, one mortally. After having several horses killed and wounded, the battery retired. There being no sign of the enemy attempting any advance, Col. DAVIS withdrew the Regiment to a more sheltered position where it remained, until night put a stop to all further work, and then marched to its bivouac of the preceding night, which proved even more cheerless than the first.

Early on the morning of the 16th while moving to our position of the previous day, messengers met us with the joyful tidings that the enemy had surrendered, which was soon made apparent by the numerous white flags seen floating over their works. The Regiment continued its march through the rebel works and into the town of Dover, where it was at once detailed to guard the immense stores left by the enemy upon the landing. Very soon Gunboats and transports arrived at the landing loaded with troops and supplies, the latter of which were very acceptable to our almost famished soldiers.

On the 17th of February the Regiment was assigned to Gen. Thayer's brigade and ordered to proceed to Fort Henry, Tenn. It was provided with two four mule teams to draw rations and cooking utensils, while the tents and all other baggage was forwarded by boat down the Cumberland and up the Tennessee rivers to Fort Henry. The Regiment arrived at Fort Henry on the afternoon of the 19th February in a terrible rainstorm and through mud indescribable. While at the Fort the Regiment occupied the log huts or barracks constructed by the Confederates, which proved most convenient and comfortable.

On the fifth of March orders were received to proceed by boat up the Tennessee River. During that afternoon and night, with great difficulty and labor, the baggage, supplies and ammunition were put on board the Steamer "Aurora." The water was very high, overflowing the banks and filling the bayous, which made it necessary to transport all the baggage to the steamer in a few small and miserably constructed boats and dug-outs, making it a very tedious as well as laborious operation.

The Regiment embarked on the 6th and started up the river on the 7th. After many delays it arrived at Savanah, Tenn., on the 12th. It laid in the vicinity of Savanah until the morning of the 18th, when it proceeded up the river, arriving at Pittsburg Landing on the same evening. March 19th, disembarked and went into camp one and a half miles from the landing, the men having to carry the greater part of their tents and baggage to camp, for the want of other means of transportation. The trip from Fort Henry to Pittsburg Landing, on account of the crowded condition of the boat, bad water, and want of proper opportunity for exercise, proved very injurious to the health of the Regiment. Several died on the way and the sick list was largely increased.

Before leaving Fort Henry the Regiment was assigned to the 2nd Brigade, 4th Division. The Brigade consisted of the 14th, 15th and 46th Illinois, and the 25th Indiana Infantry and was commanded by Col. James C. Veatch of the latter regiment. The Division was commanded by Brig. Gen. STEPHEN A. HURLBUT, of Illinois. The regiment remained quietly in camp, drilling and doing camp and picket duty, until the battle of Shiloh, on the 6th and 7th of April. On the night of the 4th of April, our camps were alarmed and our Brigade moved out about two miles to Gen. SHERMAN's camp, when we were ordered back, being told that it was a false alarm. The part taken in the battle of Shiloh by the Regiment is fully and ably set forth in the following reports, viz:

COLONEL JOHN A. DAVIS' REPORT.

HEADQUARTERS 46TH REGT. ILL. VOL. INFT'Y.
PITTSBURG LANDING, TENN., AP'L 8th, 1862.

CAPT. F. W. FOX,
Asst. Adjt. Gen'l. 2nd Brigade 4th Division.

Captain:—I have the honor to report to you that, on Sunday morning the 6th inst., at about 7½ o'clock, A. M., the enemies fire was first heard in my camp, whereupon I ordered my men to hold themselves in readiness to march at a mo: ments notice, and in less than five minutes after receiving your order my regiment was on the march to the battle-field, reaching there between 9 and 10 o'clock, A. M. It took a position ordered by Col. Veatch in person. A regiment posted about two hundred yards in front of our line gave way under the enemies fire, and retreated through my line which was lying down. As soon as it passed my men rose, dressed their line and immediately commenced pouring a destructive fire into the enemy. The regiment posted on our right gave way and the enemy, keeping up a hot fire along my whole front and a raking cross fire upon my right flank, killing and wounding over one half of my right companies, badly cutting up my other companies, eight of my line officers, the Major and color bearer wounded, I deemed it my duty, without further orders, to withdraw my command, which I did, to a position beyond the brow of a hill, where I again formed it by command of Col. Veatch. Finding no support to my right or left, I fell back to the foot of the hill, finding the 49th Illinois Infantry, commanded by Lieut. Col. Pease, at whose request I assumed command of both regiments and moved them by the right flank and established a line of battle on the ground which had been occupied by a portion of Gen. McClernand's Division, and in front of where Taylor's Battery was then planted. The enemy appearing in large force over the ground from which we had just retreated, I was ordered to withdraw my troops, that the Battery could open fire on the enemy. The 49th Ill. Infantry deployed to the left and my regiment to the right of the Battery. Forming my men again in the rear of a fence fronting the enemy, I ordered them to lay down and prepared to resist any attack the enemy might make upon the Battery.

Having succeeded in driving the enemy over the brow of the hill, the 1st Brigade of Shermans Division appeared upon the ground for the purpose of following up the enemy in their retreat. I joined my command upon the left of this Brigade and moved up in line to within two hundred yards of the enemy, when a brisk and destructive fire opened upon our whole line. Planting our colors in front of our line of battle, I ordered my command to shelter themselves behind trees and logs as best they could, within short range of the enemy, and kept up a constant fire until the regiment on our right had given away and fallen back across the ravine, when I ordered my men to fall back into the ravine, and moving them by the left flank I took them out of the range of the enemies guns. In this last engagement, Capt. Wm. Young, of company "G." who had succeeded in rallying more men after the first engagement than any other Captain, and who heroically told me he would stand by me and the colors until the last man was killed, fell, shot through the mouth, and was carried from the field. Reinforcements now arriving, and my men having been compelled to fall back from these two fierce engagements, had become somewhat scattered. It being now one o'clock, my ammunition exhausted, having lost my horse in the first engagement, and compelled to go on foot the balance of the time, and finding myself within a half mile of my Regimental encampment, I marched my men to it for dinner. Calling my men into line immediatly after dinner, I formed them on the right of the Brigade, commanded by Col. C. C. Marsh, at his request, in front of and to the left of my camp, where we again met the enemy. A Battery on my left leaving under the fire of the enemy, the regiments both on the right and left fell back, but my line did not waver, and the other regiments were again rallied and stopped the advance of the enemy.

We lay in this position on our arms all night. After breakfast in the morning, still retaining my position on the right of Col. Marsh's Brigade, I moved with him until I reached and went beyond the ground of our last engagement of Sunday, when our skirmishers were driven in and some confusion arising on the left of our Brigade, Col. Marsh ordered the Brigade to fall back and changing the whole front of his line to the left, he again moved the Brigade forward, The enemy soon drove in our pickets and we found him in strength along the whole line of our front, and when within two hundred yards the fire opened upon both sides, my men loading and firing with the coolness of veterans. Here I had another horse shot from under me in the midst of the engagement and while the battle was raging with the utmost fury. My men determined that they had fallen back for the last time, and while receiving the fire of the enemy and delivering their own with the utmost coolness, I was wounded and carried from the field. Lieut. Col. Jones reports that my men still stood firm, holding their ground, although outflanked, with the colors of the 46th and those of the rebels planted within thirty yards of each other and the enemy driven back for the last time, when the 46th was ordered, by Gen. Hurlbut in person, to their quarters.

I ought not to close this communication without bearing tribute to the gallantry and bravery of my command. Lieut. Col. Jones was with the regiment throughout all its engagements, and did his duty manfully. Maj. Dornblaser, severly wounded in the arm in the early part of the action, remained with me until the men were brought off the field and re-formed, and did not leave until after a peremptory order from myself to go to his quarters. Capt. Musser of Company "A," while his brave company was assailed by overwhelmning numbers to the front and right flank, still kept his fire pouring upon the enemy and his ranks dressed until himself wounded and carried from the field, seven of his men killed and twenty wounded in the action. The company held its ground as did all the others until ordered to retreat. Capt. Stevens while bravely keeping his men in line to bring them off the field, fell, fatally wounded, the nearest man of his company to the rebel line. Capt. Marble of Company "E," fell while brandishing his sword and calling on the Major, begged him to take it, saying, "if the rebs get me they shall not get my sword." Capt. McCracken received a severe contusion in the first engagement, but kept on duty with his company the whole of the two days. Lieuts. Hood, Barr, Arnold, Ingraham and Howell were all wounded in the first engagement of Sunday while manfully doing their duty at their posts. Too much praise cannot be awarded to the brave officers and men of the 46th Illinois Infantry who helped to win our signal victory.

All of which is respectfully submitted.

JOHN A. DAVIS,
Col. Comd'g 46th Ill. Vol. Inft'y.

LETTER OF THANKS FROM COL. C. C. MARSH.

HEADQUARTERS 2ND BRIG. 1ST DIV.,
April 9th, 1862.

DEAR SIR :—I beg to thank you and the officers and soldiers of the 46th Illinois Infantry for their noble conduct during the action of Monday morning last, when your lamented Colonel so promptly responded to my request to take a position in my command and so gallantly led you in the face of the enemy with so fatal a result to himself. My heartfelt sympathies are with you in your severe loss, and your soldierly conduct shall receive a fitting notice in my official report.

I am, sir, Truly Yours,
C. C. MARSH,
Col. 20th Ill. Inft'y, Comd'g Brigade.

EXTRACT FROM COLONEL VEATCH'S REPORT.

HEADQUARTERS 2ND BRIG. 4TH DIV.
PITTSBURG, TENN., April 10th, 1862.

CAPTAIN S. D. ATKINS,
A. A. A. Gen'l, 4th Division.

On Sunday morning while most of the troops were at breakfast, heavy firing was heard on our line in a direction suthwest from my camp. In a few moments the 2d Brigade, consisting of the 14th Illinois Infantry, Col. Hall, 15th Illinois Infantry, Lieut. Col. Ellis, 46th Illinois Infantry, Col. Davis, and 25th Indiana Infantry, Lieut. Col. Morgan, was formed in line and awaiting orders. In a short time Gen. Hurlbut's aid, Lieut. Long, directed me to move forward to support Gen. Sherman, and to take a position near a field used for reviews, beyond Col. Rap's Headquarters. When we reached the field the enemy was pressing rapidly forward toward that point. A line of battle was already formed in front of us and a second line in the rear of the first was being formed on our right. I had but little time to examine the ground, but took the best position that could be found to support the troops in front of us. An officer representing himself as acting under Gen. Sherman's orders, rode up in great haste and directed me to move my Brigade by the right flank and join to the line which was forming on our right. I executed the movement as directed but it placed the right of my Brigade on worse ground than I had chosen, though it had the advantage of forming a line of battle of greater length.

The enemy now opened fire on the troops in front of us which threw them into confusion and they broke through the lines of the 15th and 46th Illinois Infantry, many of them without returning a fire. At the same time the line on the right of this Brigade gave way and left the 15th Illinois Infantry exposed to the whole force of the enemies fire in front and a raking fire from the right. Lieut. Col. Ellis heorically held the ground and returned the fire with deadly effect. While cheering his men and directing their fire, he fell, mortally wounded. Nearly at the same time Major Goddard was killed, and the regiment, without field officers, was compelled to fall back before overpowering numbers.

The enemy was moving another heavy column on the point occupied by Col. Davis of the 46th Illinois Infantry. The line in front of him broke and rushed through his ranks, throwing them into confusion. As soon as these scattered troops had cleared his front he poured in a well directed fire upon the enemy, which for a time checked his progress, but it was impossible to hold his position against a force so far superior. Major Dornblaser was severely wounded, a large number of his company officers disabled and his color guard shot down. Col. Davis seized his colors and bore them from the field, presenting a most noted mark for the enemy who sent after him a terrific fire as he retired. I directed him to fall back and rally his men in the rear of the fresh troops that were then advancing.

* * * * * * * *

It will not be claiming too much for this Brigade to say, that, but for its determined resistance to the enemy, he would have reached the center of our camp early in the day. The field officers behaved with gallantry on every occasion.

* * * * * * * *

Col. Davis, Lieut. Col. Jones and Major Dornblaser of the 46th Illinois Infantry, each displayed coolness and courage in resisting the heavy columns thrown against them. Major Dornblaser was wounded and compelled to leave the field early on the first day. Col. Davis was severely wounded on the second day while gallantly fighting in Col. Marsh's Brigade and was carried from the field. Lieut. Col. Jones took command and conducted his regiment with skill and courage until the battle closed.

* * * * * * * *

JAMES C. VEATCH,
Colonel Commanding Brigade.

BRIG. GEN. S. A. HURLBUT'S CONGRATULATORY ORDER.

The General commanding tenders his heartfelt congratulations to the surviving officers and men of his Division, for their magnificent services during the two days of struggle which, under the blessing of God, has resulted in victory. Let the Division remember, that for five hours on Sunday they held, under the most terrific fire, the key point of the left of the army and only fell back when outflanked by overwhelming numbers, pressing through points abandoned by our supports. Let them remember, that when they fell back it was *in order*, and that the last line of resistance in rear of the heavy guns was formed first by this Division. Let them remember, that on the morning of Monday, without food and without sleep, they were ordered forward to reinforce the right, and that whenever either Brigade of this Division appeared in the field of action, they were in time to support broken planks and to hold the line. *Keep these facts in your memory*, to hand down to your children when we conquer a peace, and let it be the chief pride of every man in the command—as it is of your General—that he was at Pittsburg with the FIGHTING FOURTH DIVISION.

By Order of
BRIG. GEN. S. A. HURLBUT:

SMITH D. ATKINS,
   A. A. A. Gen'l, 4th Division.

During the two days fighting at Shiloh, the regiment lost one hundred and ninety-six men killed, wounded and missing.

Prior to the battle, Col. Davis obtained sufficient transportation for the regiment, it having been in the field nearly two months without the means of transporting rations or baggage except what was carried by the men.

On the 24th of April, the regiment with the Brigade, commenced its march upon Corinth, Miss. The first day it marched but four miles and went into camp, from which it did not again move until the 30th of April. On the 29th of April Major Hazelton, Paymaster U. S. A., paid the regiment up to February 28th, being the first pay that it had received since its organization. On the 30th of April the old Fourth Division made its famous march through Monterey, Tenn. Although the distance made was but five miles, it was a very hard day's march through such a rain storm and over such roads as will never be forgotten. The teams with the baggage and supplies could not get through until the following day. The regiment went into camp at Pea Ridge, where it remained until the fourth of May, when it again advanced a few miles. Skirmishing with the enemy now commenced, they disputing our way almost constantly. On the eighth of

May we advanced two miles toward Corinth, driving the enemy and capturing some prisoners and property. On the 9th the rebel pickets were pressed back nearly three miles, and on the 10th our camp was taken to the front. Our lines were thus advanced from day to day with more or less skirmishing until the 14th of May, when the work of throwing up heavy lines of eathworks was commenced in good earnest and the siege of Corinth actually began.

On the 21st of May another advance was made, and another line of works thrown up. On the 27th the 46th Illinois Infantry was sent around to the rear of Corinth with a large force of Cavalry, on a reconnoisance. Near Purdy Church the enemy was encountered by the advance guard of cavalry.

The 46th was at once ordered to the front, one company ("A.") was deployed as skirmishers and the remainder formed into line as fast as they could come up. The enemy soon appeared upon a full charge, but after receiving a volly from the skirmishers, turned and fled in great confusion, with a loss to them of eight killed and wounded and no loss to us. The object of the expedition having been accomplished, we returned to camp very much fatigued by our long and rapid march. The particular object of sending one small regiment of Infantry on a scout with over three thousand cavalry, and when the enemy was encountered, hurrying the Infantry forward on the run to the front, could never be fully comprehended by the combined wisdom of the regiment.

On the 29th our lines were again advanced three fourths of a mile, and a line of heavy works thrown up. Early on the morning of the 30th, it was discovered that the enemy had evacuated Corinth during the previous day and night, thus enabling our army to take peaceable possession of the town.

On the 2d of June we broke camp and marched through Corinth, and went into camp six miles west from the town. On the 9th the regiment was again paid by Major Phelps, for March and April. On the 10th marched fifteen miles to Hatchie River and constructed a bridge across the same on the 11th, which had been destroyed by the rebels to retard our pursuit. Our march was leisurely continued until Sunday, June 15th, when we passed through Grand Junction, Tenn., and went into camp at Cold Springs, three miles southwest from Grand Junction. Here the regiment did its first drilling since the battle of Shiloh, its music consisting of one snare and one base drum. On the 24th we moved our camp four miles to a point two miles west of La Grange. The place of our encampment here is known by the regiment as "Collar Bone Hill."

June 30th, left camp at 2 p. m., and marched twelve miles to old "Lamar Church" in the direction of Holly Springs, Miss. July 1st, marched to Cold Water Creek. It was reported that the rebels had a camp at this place, but we found no enemy and went into camp. On the 3d we had a big scare, which brought us into line in a remarkably short space of time. It was reported that the enemy were advancing upon us in large force, but after making a more cool and accurate reconnoisance it proved a false alarm, being one of our own regiments coming in from a scout.

On the 5th of July, we commenced our return march, having accomplished all that was expected. We returned by the same route we came and arrived at La Grange on the 6th. The heat was intense on our return march, and water poor and scarce, causing much suffering. A number of men in the command were sun-struck.

On the 17th of July we struck tents and commenced our march to Memphis, Tenn., going to Moscow the first day, to Lafayette the second, to Germantown the third, to Whites' Station the fourth, and on the fifth day, July 21st, to camp two miles South of Memphis, on the east bank of the Mississippi River.

The distance from La Grange to Memphis is fifty miles, and the march was made in the hottest weather and over the most dusty roads. The regiment had been unable to procure new clothes for a long time and its appearance when entering the city of Memphis called forth anything but complimentary remarks as to its dress. Several officers had to substitute their last pair of drawers for pants. Jew clothing dealers went into ecstacies of delight as they saw the ragged column pass in anticipation of large sales and larger profits.

The regiment was engaged in camp and picket duty until August 27th, when it went with the Brigade on a scout on the "Pigeon Roost" road running southeast from Memphis to Nonconah Creek, six miles from Memphis, and encamped. On the 29th went two miles further, the cavalry going in advance, capturing some twenty-five prisoners. Returned to camp on the 31st, having accomplished but little.

On the 6th of September, the whole Division started in the direction of Brownsville, Tenn., to which place it was supposed we were ordered. We had orders to be ready to march at 2, a. m., consequently the men were aroused at one o'clock, tents struck and wagons loaded, but the order to march did not come until four o'clock p. m. We marched through the city and encamped for the night near Wolf river, five miles from Memphis. On the 7th, marched sixteen miles through Raleigh and Union Station on the M. & C. R. R. Rested on the 8th. September 9th, marched to Big Muddy River,—a very appropriate name—where the bridge had been destroyed by the rebels. After constructing a crossing so as to enable us to resume our march, a messenger arrived with orders for us to proceed to Bolivar, Tenn., instead of Brownsville. Hence on the 11th we moved by the way of Hampton Station and Danville, and on the 12th through Whiteville to Pleasant Creek, three miles northeast of Bolivar. On the 14th we changed camp, passing through Bolivar to the Hatchie river, two miles north of town. We were obliged to change our camp every few days from one side of the town to the other until the 24th of September. On the 27th of September all the troops of this place were reviewed by Generals McPherson, Veatch and Lauman. They made a very fine appearance.

While here Colonel John A. Davis returned to the regiment and was very warmly greeted. He had been absent since the battle of Shiloh, suffering from a severe wound, which still troubled him.

On the 4th of October orders were received to proceed towards Corinth to make a division in favor of our force there, which had been attacked by Price and Van Dorn. When near Matamora on Hatchie river, a large force of rebels were encountered and vigorously attacked by our forces, soon driving them across the river, capturing several pieces of artillery and a large number of prisoners. The part taken by the 46th Illinois in this engagement is fully given in the following report:

LIEUT. COL. JOHN J. JONES' REPORT.

HEADQUARTERS 46TH ILLS. VOL. INFT'Y.
BOLIVAR, TENN., Oct. 9th, 1862.

CAPTAIN F. W. Fox,
A. A. Gen'l 2nd Brig. 4th Division.

Captain.—At eight o'clock on the morning of the 5th inst., under orders from Brig. Gen. Veatch, the 46th regiment took a position on the right of the 2d Brigade, in the advance, to support Bolton's Battery, two miles west of the Big Hatchie. After firing shots the Battery took a position half a mile in advance, where they opened a galling fire upon the rebels, which lasted about three-fourths of an hour, when the word "forward" was given. The men all moved at the word and soon received the melancholy intelligence that our loved and gallant Col. Davis was again severely wounded by a canister shot. When I took command and announced this, the regiment seemed determined to avenge their loss, and soon an opportunity offered, for at this moment the rebels opened their first volly at short range, which was received with great coolness by the men until they heard the command to fire which they did and charged, driving the rebels over and from their batteries to the opposite bank of the river. Here the enemy made a stand, and confidently expected to repulse our force, but the word was still "forward," and on we marched at double-quick, forming in line over the river. Here Sergeant John E. Hershey, color bearer, fell wounded. Corpl. Thomas E. Joiner, of company "G," true to duty, bore both colors across the field and handed one to Priv. James Hobdey, of company "I," who done it honor through the day. At this time Captain F. W. Fox, of General Veatch's Staff, took the front and called the 46th to follow him, when the regiment charged with cheer after cheer, until the field was theirs. In the last line formed, about four o'clock, p. m., the brave and generous Lt. Moses R. Thompson fell mortally wounded. I cannot close this report without special mention of Assistant Surgeon Benj. H. Bradshaw, who, unassisted, took the wounded from amid the ranks, doing even more than his duty; also the officers of the line, who were all at their posts, fearless of rebel power, and if honor has been won it is due to them and their brave men alone. Herewith is a report of the killed and wounded of my command.

Very Respectfully, Your Ob't Serv't,
JOHN J. JONES,
Lieutenant Colonel Commanding

Brig. Gen. Veatch in his report of the battle of the Hatchie, speaks in the highest terms of his Brigade. He says: "The field and staff officers of every regiment appeared to do all that could be done to render victory complete. The line officers, so far as their conduct came within my notice, did their whole duty, and the men moved with steadiness and resolute courage not easily surpassed. The loss in killed and wounded embraces many valuable officers. Col. John A. Davis of the 46th Illinois infantry, fell severely wounded early in the action while gallantly leading his regiment in a charge. He has since died of his wounds. He was generous, noble and brave, and will be regretted by all who knew him."

GENERAL VEATCH'S CONGRATULATORY ORDER.

HEADQUARTERS 2ND BRIGADE 4TH DIVISION,
BOLIVAR, TENN., Oct. 9th, 1862.

GENERAL ORDERS,
No. 62.

The General desires to congratulate the troops of his command on the brilliant victory of the battle of the Hatchie. On no field since the war began has better fighting been done. The force of the enemy greatly superior in numbers, were posted in the very strongest positions, and commanded by those veteran Generals Van Dorn and Price. You met them, you fought them, you drove them, you defeated and routed them, capturing a battery and hundreds of prisoners. You compelled them to seek shelter on the east side of the Hatchie. Here the 1st Baigade came to your support and with Hurlbut's fighting fourth Division united, you drove them again from their last stronghold and forced them to a hasty retreat. While we rejoice in victory we regret the loss of many brave men. Let us honor the memory of our fallen comrades, and transmit to their friends the story of their noble deeds. The wounded who survive will carry their battle scars which will speak more eloquently for their bravery and daring than words can do.

A battery of four field pieces captured by this brigade has been entrusted to your care by the Major General commanding the Division. These pieces, manufactured in rebel workshops, will be made to do service for the Union in the hands of Bolton and Burnap.

Officers and men of the 2d Brigade! You have the confidence of your Generals, and the respect and esteem of all loyal citizens. Let your future good conduct maintain the high reputation you have gained. Remember that you belong to "Hurlbut's Fighting Fourth Division;" that what he commands you will obey; what he orders you will execute; where he leads you will follow with full confidence of honor and victory.

By Order of Brig. Gen. JAMES C VEATCH:

F. W. Fox, A. A. Gen'l.

After the battle the regiment returned to its camp at Bolivar, Tenn. Col. John A. Davis and Lieutenant Moses R. Thompson died of their wounds on the 10th of October, and their remains sent home for burial. Both were men of the highest worth and standing at home. Both entered the service with the purest motives, and both received their death wounds while bravely and nobly fighting at their posts. Their memories will ever be kindly cherished.

On the 3d of November, the regiment with the Brigade, marched to La Grange, Tenn., via Grand Junction, and went into the old camp at La Grange, where we remained till the 28th of November, nothing noteworthy occurring excepting a few Grand Reviews. We then took up our line of march to Holly Springs, Miss., where we arrived on the night of the 29th. November 30th marched south toward the Tallehatchie River, and went into camp near Waterford, twelve miles south of Holly Springs. The enemy abandoned his works on the Tallehatchie and retreated towards Oxford. We remained in camp, in an old cornfield, which became extremely muddy during the heavy rains, until the 9th of December, when we changed our camp to a fine wood two miles south, where it was almost universally supposed we should remain for the winter; hence, on the 10th our grounds were put in splendid condition, tents pitched in line, chimneys built and our camp christened "Camp Hall," when suddenly all our plans were frustrated by an order to be ready to march at seven a. m., the next day. December 11th, marched twenty miles to Hurricane Creek, six miles from Oxford, and the next day eleven miles beyond Oxford to the vicinity of Yoncona Station on the Mississippi Central R. R., where we remained until December 22d, when we marched five miles to Taylor's Station on the same road.

Van Dorn having captured Holly Springs and cut off our communication, our forces marched north again on the 23d, through Oxford to Hurricane Creek, a distance of seventeen miles and arriving at noon: On the 24th the 46th Illinois and 33d Wisconsin Infantry, in command of Colonel Moore, left Hurricane Creek in charge of the corps train, arriving safe on the north side of the Tallchatchie late on the same night. We remained in this camp until the 26th of December, making Christmas as merry as the means at our command would permit, when we moved our camp four miles nearer Holly Springs, between Waterford and Wyatt Stations on the Mississippi Central Railroad.

Here the new year of 1863 was duly inaugurated with a feast, the best the country could afford, which was our whole dependence, as Uncle Sam's commissary had ceased to honor requisitions. The feast consisted of *corn* in all the varieties of style known to experienced camp cooks, except corn in the *juice*. However, the New Year's Day was not the least happy one.

On the 6th of January, we marched to Holly Springs, where we remained to the 10th, when the 15th and 46th Illinois Infantry were ordered to escort the ammunition train to La Grange Tenn., at which place we arrived late on the night of the 11th of January. Our progress was very slow and tedious on account of muddy roads and emaciated condition of the mules attached to the train.

On the 13th of January, we marched to Moscow, Tenn., nine miles west of La Grange. Remained at Moscow doing guard duty until February 5th, when we went to La Fayette, Tenn., eight miles west. The garrison at Moscow up to this time consisted of the 1st Brigade, 4th Division, and the 46th and 76th Illinois Infantry of the 2d Brigade, and two batteries. After re-joining the Brigade at La Fayette and performing similar duties as at Moscow until the 9th of March, we marched via Collierville and Germantown to Memphis, Tenn., arriving at the latter place on the 12th. We went into camp on the northeast side of the city, near the fair ground, which made quite an extensive as well as beautiful drill ground.

On the 21st of April the 46th, 14th Illinois Infantry, and 5th Ohio Battery were sent out to re-enforce Colonel Bryant of the 12th Wisconsin Infantry, who had gone in the direction of Hernando, Miss., with a Brigade and met the enemy in force near Cold Water. He then moved his whole force again three miles south of Hernando and encamped for the night, as the cavalry had reported the enemy gone. Colonel Bryant had captured and sent to Memphis about seventy prisoners and a large lot of mules and horses. April 23d, commenced our return march to Memphis, where we arrived on the 24th, thoroughly drenched by a heavy rain. We met with no loss and the troops made the march in good time and in fine order. We remained in camp at Memphis until the 13th of May, when we embarked on the Steamer "Clara Poe," and left the same evening for Vicksburg, Miss. Passed Helena on the morning of the 14th and Napoleon at six o'clock p. m., same day. Private Gottlieb Vohmer, "C" Co. fell overboard during the night and was drowned. As we passed Gaines' Landing, Arkansas, the Steamer "Fort Wayne," with the 76th Illinois Infantry on board, was fired into by guerillas from the Arkansas shore. Three men were wounded and the boat disabled by running foul of some drift wood, breaking the wheel and rudder. We reached Young's Point, La., at 8 p. m., May 15th. Disembarked on the 16th and went into camp near the landing. At eleven o'clock a. m., on the 18th, we marched across the Point to Bower's Landing, below Vicksburg, leaving all our tents and baggage at Sherman's Landing. On the next day a portion of the Brigade embarked and went to Grand Gulf, but the 46th and the two Batteries belonging to the Brigade were obliged to await the return of the transports that had taken the other troops. Before their return, however, orders were received by us to return at once to Sherman's Landing, as General Grant had opened communication via the Yazoo River to the troops in the rear of Vicksburg. Arrived at Sherman's Landing on the night of the 19th, and at noon on the 20th embarked on the Steamer "Luminary," and proceeded up the Yazoo river to Chickasaw Bayou. Disembarked and moved three miles in a southeasterly direction across the swamps to the bluff.

On the 21st of May the balance of the Brigade joined us and proceeded to the right of Gen. Grant's lines about the city. We were at once ordered to Snyder's Bluffs on the Yazoo river, ten miles from Vicksburg. Went into camp at the Bluffs on the same evening, much disappointed that we were not permitted to enter the line of attack. The object of sending us to this place was to watch a large rebel force said to be advancing to form a junction with the Vicksburg garrison.

On the 24th of May we marched in the direction of Vicksburg on the Benton road. The road was extremely dry and dusty and the weather very warm, making it a very hard march. On the 25th we marched to the extreme left of our lines near the Mississippi river, below Vicksburg, and relieved Gen. McArthur's Division. The regiment was detailed for picket duty, and during the night one wing was surrounded and one hundred and thirteen officers and men captured by the enemy. The particulars of the capture are set forth in the following reports, viz:

HEADQUARTERS 46TH ILL. VOL. INFANTRY.
IN THE FIELD, June 7th, 1863.

S. P. BOURQUIN,
   A. A. A. General :

Lieutenant :—In compliance with orders from Division Headquarters, with reference to a capture of a portion of the 46th Illinois Infantry, I have the honor to report that on the afternoon of the 25th of May, the regiment was detailed to relieve the 63d Illinois Infantry on picket duty. At 4 o'clock p. m., the regiment reported at Brigade Headquarters, but owing to unavoidable difficulties the regiment was not fully posted until after 7 o'clock p. m. Five componies—a portion of which were captured—were posted by Lieut. Col. John J. Jones of my regiment, under the guidance of the Major of the 63d Illinois Infantry, and upon the same ground in the same manner that the 63d was posted at the time we relieved them, which line extended from and near a cotton gin on the Warrenton road westward to a swamp which we supposed and had been informed was impassable. The other portion of the regiment was posted from the Warrenton road eastward to the pickets of the 1st Brigade by myself, but owing to the lateness of the hour when I arrived at the center of our lines, and having implicit confidence in the ability and skill of Lieut. Col. Jones and other officers on that portion of the line, I deemed it entirely unnecessary to visit it. The first alarm occurred at about half past nine o'clock p. m. I heard several sharp volleys of musketry. I immediately strengthened the several posts nearest the point of alarm, and proceeded in person to the point from whence the alarm came, to discover, if possible, the cause. I had gone but a short distance when I discovered a body of troops moving rapidly along a skirt of timber towards the river, which proved to be rebel soldiers. Owing to the extended line of pickets, I had only men enough to hold that portion of the line east of the Warrenton road. Unable to hear anything from the pickets on the west side of the road, and fearing some disaster had befallen them, I immediately deployed skirmishers along the Warrenton road, which afforded them a full view of the ground between it and the river bluff, in order to guard against a flank movement of the enemy with a view to cut us off and capture us. At the earliest opportunity, I notified the Brigade commanders, Col. Hall and Col. McGowan, commanding a Brigade in Gen. McArthur's Division, who both rendered me prompt assistance. For more full and complete particulars, I refer you to the reports of officers of my command enclosed herewith.

As to the degree of vigilance exercised by the officers and men of my command, I can only speak of those under my own control, which met with my entire approbation, and from the known character of the officers in charge of the captured portion of the regiment, with possibly one excep-

tion, which I have not yet sufficient information to report, I believe the disaster to be more attributable to an injudicious posting of the pickets than to a lack of vigilance.
   Very Respectfully, Your Ob't Sv't.
      B. DORNBLASER, Col. Comd'g Reg't.

The remainder of the regiment took a very active part in the siege of Vicksburg, from the 25th of May until its surrender on the 4th of July, doing picket duty both in the front and rear, digging trenches, &c., &c.

The 4th of July will be kept in sacred remembrance by all who took part in the famous siege of Vicksburg.

On the afternoon of July 4th, orders were received to keep our men in camp and prepare for a march. Next morning the Division left camp and proceeded to Clear Creek, twelve miles east of Vicksburg on the Vicksburg and Jackson railroad. The day was extremely warm and the roads very dusty. July 6th, marched through Edward's Station to near Bolton's Station, twenty miles. We marched part of the night until the rainstorm made the roads impassable, which, with the extreme darkness, rendered further progress out of the question. The only shelter we had from the driving storm was a rail fence, which afforded both warmth and shelter. July 7th, marched three miles and encamped until dusk, then resumed our march in the rear of the corps train until twelve o'clock and bivouacked until morning. July 8th, marched to Clinton, and on the 9th the Brigade was detailed to guard the train to Jackson, Miss. Marched six miles and parked the train on Dickson's plantation, where we remained in charge of the train until the afternoon of the 12th, when we were ordered to proceed to Jackson and report for orders to Gen. A. P. Hovey, Gen. Lauman having been relieved of the command of the 4th Division after making his disastrous charge upon the enemies works.

The 46th Illinois Infantry was posted on the extreme right of our line, near Pearl river south of Jackson. Earthworks were thrown up in front of the regiment and a battery placed in position to command both front and flank. Our 4th Division was temporarily assigned to the 12th Division 13th Army Corps, commanded by Gen. A. P. Hovey. The siege was actively carried on from the 12th to the 16th of July, when the enemy evacuated the place. The regiment did its full share of the work.

COL. HALL'S REPORT OF THE SECOND BRIGADE.

HEADQUARTERS 4TH BRIGADE 12TH DIVISION.
JACKSON, MISS., JULY, 1863.

CAPTAIN PHILIPS:
A. A. Gen'l., 12th Division, 13th Army Corps.

Captain:—I have the honor to report to you the part taken by my command, consisting of the 14th, 15th, 46th and 76th Illinois Infantry, Co. "K," 2d Illinois Artillery, and 4th Ohio Battery, before the fortified city of Jackson.

Late on the p. m. of the 12th instant, whilst encamped at Dickson's plantation five miles west of Jackson, I received orders from Major General E. O. C. Ord, commanding 13th Army Corps, directing me to report to Brig. Gen. A. P. Hovey, commanding 12th Division 13th Army Corps, for orders, which order I obeyed as speedily as possible, arriving at Gen. Hovey's Headquarters at nine o'clock p. m. At 4 o'clock a. m., I put the column in motion and took a position on a ridge on the east side of the New Orleans and Jackson railroad, which position we immediately proceeded to entrench and put in the best possible state of defense.

On the morning of the 15th, I was ordered by Gen. Hovey to send scouts from my right east to Pearl River, which duty was performed by 2d Lieut. Reed and six men from company "I," 15th Illinois Infantry, in a very able and satisfactory manner, finding the enemy in force on the east side, with one company on the west side as pickets. After making known to Gen. Hovey the disposition of the enemy's force, I was ordered to take the 15th, 46th and 76th Illinois Infantry and make a rapid move on the enemy at the river. The move was made with great rapidity, but not sufficiently so as to overtake the enemy. We reached the river just in time to see the last of their pickets pass out of sight on the opposite bank.

On the morning of the 16th it became apparent to some of the officers of my command that the enemy was evacuating Jackson, which fact I at once communicated to Gen. Hovey, it being the first intimation he had of it.

The spirit manifested by both officers and men during the short siege was highly commendable, obeying with alacrity every order, and executing the work assigned them with zeal and enthusiasm. To Col. B. Dornblaser and Capt. R. P. McKnight, A. A. G. of this Brigade, I am particularly indebted for valuable information obtained by reconoitering the enemy's works.

Respectfully your Obedient Servant,
CYRUS HALL.
Colonel Commanding Brigade.

On the night of the 16th of July, the rebels evacuated the

town and retreated rapidly toward Meridian, leaving us to take quiet possession on the 17th. After pursuing the enemy and destroying the railroad and other public property in and about Jackson, the troops commenced their return march on the 21st, via Raymond and Big Black Bridge to Vicksburg, where we arrived at one p. m. on the 23d, having marched over fifty miles in two days and a half, through terrible heat and dust.

The Division was again detached from the 12th Division, and placed in command of Brig. Gen. M. M. Crocker, and soon after transferred to the 17th Army Corps by General Orders No. 214, Department Headquarters. August 11th, 1863, embarked on Steamer "Rocket," and left on the morning of the 12th for Natchez, Miss., where we arrived the next morning. The regiment at once disembarked and went into camp one and a half miles from the city, northeast, where it remained doing camp and garrison duty until September 1st, when it started out with the Division on an expedition into Louisiana. The following is a report of the same:

REPORT OF EXPEDITION INTO LOUISIANA.

HEADQUARTERN 46TH ILL. INFT'Y VOLS.
NATCHEZ, MISS., Sept. 8th, 1863.

CAPTAIN R. P. McKNIGHT,
A. A. Genl 2d Brig. 4th Div. 17th Army Corps.

Captain :—I have the honor to report that the regiment left this camp at.12 m., September 1st, and marched with the Brigade, in the place assigned it by your order, to the Mississippi river at Natchez. Crossed over in transports and encamped for the night at Vidalia, La. Early on the 2d it took up its line of march at the Head of the Brigade, and marched sixteen miles to the west side of Cross Bayou, going into camp at sundown. On the 3d, marched to Trinity on the Washita river twelve miles, arriving there a little past noon. By your order the 46th and 76th Illinois Infantry, both under my command, were left at this place to guard the trains and ferry, whilst the balance of the force proceeded to Harrisonburg, La. Upon your return on the 5th, the regiment was ordered to escort a part of the artillery and Brigade train to Cross Bayou, ferry the same across and select the camp for the night for the Brigade; all of which was safely accomplished by eight o'clock p. m.

On the 6th the regiment marched with the Brigade to Vidalia, crossed the river and arrived in this camp at five o'clock p. m. The march was made without los or incident worthy of special note. The officers and men of my command acquitted themselves as good soldiers throughout.

I am, Captain, very Respectfully,
B. DORNBLASER,
Col. Commanding Regiment.

The regiment immediately resumed its usual routine of camp and picket duty, interspersed with prize inspections and drills, together with occassional reviews by our commanding General and distinguished military visitors, which made our stay at the beautiful city of Natchez both pleasant and profitable.

On the 10th of November the regiment embarked for Vicksburg, where we arrived on the evening of the 11th; disembarked and bivouacked on the levee for the night and the next day located our camp near the Vicksburg cemetery. We had to occupy old camps. covered with all kinds of filth and rubbish, and only sufficiently large to accomodate a half a regiment comfortably. However, our stay in this camp, fortunately, was not of long duration.

On the 28th of November we moved camp to Camp Cowan, near Clear Creek, nine miles from Vicksburg. Here the construction of comfortable log barracks was immediately commenced and soon completed, making it one of the most pleasant and comfortable camps it has ever been our good fortune to occupy.

About the time our barracks were completed General Orders No. 191, A. G. O , Washington, D. C., relating to re-enlisting Veteran Volunteers was received. Vigerous measures were at once adopted by the officers of the regiment to reenlist the same as a veteran regiment. The enlisted men came forward with great unanimity and promptness. On the 4th of January, 1864, three-fourths of the regiment was mustered into the service of the United States for three years or during the war, by Lieut. C. W. G. Hyde, A. C. M., 4th Division, 17th Army Corps, and on the tenth of January Gen. McPherson ordered the regiment to proceed to Vicksburg and embark on the Steamer "Planet," then awaiting us.

On the evening of the 11th the regiment was paid by Major Stewart on board of the boat, and the next day at nine and a half o'clock a. m., the regiment, numbering twenty officers and three hundred and thirty-four enlisted men, left Vicksburg for the North to enjoy a thirty days' furlough and to fill up the regiment if possible.

The river as far up as Napoleon, Arkansas, was full of floating ice, which greatly impeded our progress. We passed Napoleon at six o'clock a. m. of the 15th, Helena at two o'clock and fifteen minutes on the 16th, arriving at Memphis on the same evening at nine o'clock. Left Memphis on the 17th at six o'clock p. m., and arrived at Cairo, Illinois, on the 20th at 11 o'clock a. m. Col. Dornblaser at once telegraphed to Col. Allen C. Fuller, Adjutant General, at Springfield, Illinois, who ordered us to proceed direct to Freeport, Illinois, as our place of rendezvous.

By reason of want of railroad transportation, the regiment was obliged to remain on the boat until noon of the 22d, when it proceeded by special train on the Illinois Central R. R. to Freeport, Illinois, where it arrived at half past twelve o'clock p. m. on the 23d of January. The citizens of Freeport and vicinity gave the regiment a most hearty and enthusiastic reception, which will ever be remembered gratefully by every officer and soldier in the 46th.

After marching through some of the principal streets of the city, and listening to some eloquent welcoming speeches, the regiment stacked arms in the streets and entered Plymouth Hall, where a most sumptuous repast awaited them, prepared by the fair ladies of Freeport and vicinity. When the boys appetites were appeased they again fell into line and marched to the barracks on the fair ground one mile west of the city.

Adjutant Woodbury had gone direct to Springfield from Cairo to procure the furloughs for the men. He arrived at Freeport on the 26th and on the 27th the whole regiment was furloughed for thirty days, when it would again assemble at Camp Freeport.

Recruiting stations were established and recruiting officers appointed in Lee, Ogle, Whiteside and Stephenson Counties, and the work of filling up the regiment vigorously commenced with flattering prospects of success.

The regiment has thus far made a name for itself of which it feels proud, and the noble State in which it in part represents has never been dishonored by it. When it again returns to the field with full ranks, it will doubtless add still brighter lustre to its name, and continue as heretofore to be an honor to the State.

PART SECOND.

From the 27th of January till the 1st of March, the officers and men of the regiment vied with each other in laudable efforts to fill up the same. The nine old companies were mostly filled up, and Capt. Crane of Freeport, Illinois, had recruited and organized a new company ("D,") for the regiment by authority of the War Department.

On the 2d day of March the regiment left Freeport with an aggregate of 987 men, and proceeded to Cairo, Illinois, by rail, thence to Vicksburg, Miss., by boat; thence to Camp Hebron, ten miles east from Vicksburg, and re-joined the 2d Brigade 4th Division, 17th Army Corps. From March 10th until April 5th, the regiment was vigorously drilled and fitted for active service in the field. On the latter date the Brigade marched to Big Black Bridge, twelve miles east from Vicksburg, and reported to Brig. Gen. E. S. Dennis, commanding. April 25th the regiment moved by rail to Vicksburg, and encamped near Battery Ransom, northeast of the city, doing garrison duty. May 4th we started on an expedition to Benton and Yazoo City, Miss., commanded by Brig. Gen. John McArthur, and returned to camp at Vicksburg on the 21st of May..

REPORT OF THE EXPEDITION.

HEADQ'RS 1ST BRIGADE YAZOO EXPEDITION,
VICKSBURG, MISS,, May 22d, 1864.

CAPTAIN W. F. RANDALL:
Assistant Adjutant General.

Captain:—I have the honor to submit the following report of the part taken by this Brigade in the Yazoo expedition:

At five o'clock a. m. of the 4th inst., the 1st Brigade, consisting of the 46th Illinois Infantry, Lieut. Col. John J. Jones commanding, and the 76th Illinois Infantry, Col. Samuel T. Busey commanding, left camp and proceeded via Jackson road to Hebron, Mechanicsville and Benton, which we reached on the 7th. The enemy seemed disposed to dispute our possession of the place. The 1st Brigade marching in the rear was ordered up, leaving two companies with the train, and formed by your order in a field east of the town and in the rear of the 124th Illinois Infantry of the 2d Brigade. The enemy, however, soon fled before our advance and left our troops in quiet possession of the place.

On the morning of the 8th General McArthur went to Yazoo city to communicate with General Slocum at Vicksburg, leaving me in command during his absence. At about two o'clock p. m. of the 9th, a scout reported the enemy advancing in large force on the Lexington road. I at once formed my Brigade and Boltons Battery on that road and requested Col. Coats of the 2d Brigade to form it on the Canton road, which was promptly done. Major Mumford with his 5th Illinois Cavalry dismounted, passed around my left, deployed as skirmishers and drove the enemy across to the old Lexington road, from which a few well directed shots from Bolton's Battery drove them pell mell into the timber beyond the field. Major Cook of the 3d U. S. Cavalry, (colored) with a portion of his command, also drove to the shelter of the woods a small force of the enemy who were advancing via Pickett's plantation towards the right of my Brigade. After posting a strong picket, I ordered the troops to camp.

On the morning of the 12th, I was ordered by General McArthur to remain at Benton to guard the approaches by the Lexington road with the 1st Brigade and one section of Bolton's Battery, whilst he with the other troops went to Moore's Ferry, on the Big Black, via the Canton road, on a reconnoisance, returning the same day. At five o'clock a. m, on the 13th, the expedition started for Vaughan's Station on the Mississippi Central Railroad, the 1st Brigade in the advance. The cavalry advance encountered the enemy at Luce's plantation, five miles southeast from Benton. I ordered the 76th Illinois forward to support a section of artillery commanded by Lieut. Nichols, who, together with a line of skirmishers from the 76th Illinois Infantry, drove the enemy from their position. The column then moved forward in its regular order of march along the road about one and a half miles, when the enemy was again found posted in a strong position with three pieces of artillery. I at once pushed my Brigade forward to an open field, forming the 76th on the left and the 46th Illinois Infantry on the right of the road, throwing forward two companies each as skirmishers, while at the same time Lieut. Nichols, with a section of artillery posted on the right of the road near the timber, opened a vigorous and well directed fire upon the rebels' battery, which was soon silenced and compelled to retreat. I then moved forward in line of battle with skirmishers well advanced—expecting to encounter the enemy at any moment—fully a mile to the plantation houses where I halted to await orders. The General commanding, finding the enemy gone, permitted the troops to rest and refresh themselves after their weary march.

After a halt of an hour and a half, the column again moved forward to within two miles of Vaughan's Station and encamped for the night, the enemy making but a feeble resistance to our advance. On the 14th we moved via Decenville to Benton, and on the 15th to Yazoo City, where we remained until the morning of the 18th, when we proceeded via Liverpool, Sartatia and Haine's Bluffs to camp at Vicksburg, where we arrived at ten o'clock a. m., having marched over two hundred miles.

The only casualty I have to report in my command, is that of Sergeant Eells, company "D," 46th Illinois Infantry, who was killed on the morning of the 14th while acting as a scout, for which he was well suited, and in which capacity he had rendered much valuable service.

Although the march was a long one and rendered wearisome by the heat and dust, but very few complaints were heard, and whenever a fight was expected every man was found in his place ready and eager for the fray.

The officers of this command, including my personal staff, are entitled to great praise for the able and prompt discharge of every duty devolving upon them.

I have the honor to be, Sir,
Very Respectfully, your Obe't Serv't,
B. DORNBLASER,
Colonel Commanding Brigade.

The regiment remained quietly in camp, drilling and performing picket and camp duty until the 1st of July, when it went out with another expedition, commanded by Major General Slocum.

REPORT OF THE JACKSON EXPEDITION.

HEADQUARTERS 2ND BRIG. 4TH DIV., 17TH A. C.,
VICKSBURG, Miss., July 13, 1865.

CAPT. W. E. KUHN.

A. A. A. Gen'l, 1st Div., 17th A. C.

Captain :—I have the honor to submit the following report of the part taken by this Brigade in the late expedition to Jackson, Miss., and return.

In compliance with orders from Brig. Gen. E. S. Dennis, commanding 1st Division, the Brigade consisting of the 46th Illinois Infantry, Lieutenant Col. Jones commanding, and the 76th Illinois Infantry, Col. Samuel T. Busey commanding, left camp at 3 A. M. on 1st instant, and proceeded to Big Black Bridge, where we had to await supplies and the building of a pontoon bridge across Big Black. Left Big Black on the morning of the third, and reached Clinton on the 4th inst. at noon, meeting with but little opposition from the enemy. During the afternoon quite a large force of rebels took a position about one and a half miles east of Clinton, on the Jackson road, and made several sallies on the pickets.

Early on the morning of the 5th inst., the enemy was encountered by the advance, and driven back to within three and a half miles of Jackson, when they made a stand, using several pieces of artillery with great skill and accuracy. The 76th and five companies of the 11th Illinois Infantry guarded the train. Col. Coates moved his Brigade by a circutous route to the left to gain the enemies flank. At the same time, by Gen. Slocum's order, I moved the 46th and four pieces of artillery commanded by Lieut. Moore through a thick belt of timber, on the left of the Jackson road, thereby gaining a commanding position, and by a few well directed shots from the Battery, drove what was left of the enemy, from the ground. I advanced with the force at my command and occupied the rebel position without further opposition. After resting several hours to enable the other troops to come up, the Brigade marched into Jackson in splendid order and encamped on the south side of the city.

At four P. M. of the 6th, the troops left Jackson on the same road they came; the cavalry in advance followed by this Brigade. Near the Junction of the Clinton and Canton roads, three miles from Jackson, and near where the enemy was posted the day before, they were discovered advancing in heavy force, evidently with the intention of gaining a position to prevent us leaving by this route. Major Mumford with his cavalry attacked them with great spirit, and held them in check until this Brigade could be brought up to his support. Forming the 46th Illinois Infantry on the right of the Canton road, and the 76th Illinois Infantry on the left, with Lieut. Nichols' section of Artillery in the center, I advanced under a heavy fire about a half a mile. Here Lt. Nichols posted his section, supported by the 76th and opened a vigorous fire upon the enemy; while the 46th moved forward and took a position on a hill farther in advance, and within short range of the enemy's line. A brisk fire was kept up on both sides until darkness closed the work. During the engagement Capt. Clingman of A Co., 46th Illinois Infantry, was severely wounded through the left arm. Lieut. Moore made repeated attempts to plant his section of Artillery in advance near the 46th, but found every prominent point so completely commanded by the sharp-shooters, that he was compelled reluctantly to withdraw. After posting a strong picket, I ordered the Brigade back to a less exposed position and encamped for the night.

Next morning at four o'clock, by order of Major Gen. Slocum I moved the Brigade across a field in a Northwesterly direction to take possession of a house held by the enemy on the previous evening, to enable our train to pass out on the Clinton road. The leading Regiment, the 76th Illinois, had advanced but a short distance beyond our position of the previous evening when it was brought to a stand by a heavy force of the enemy strongly posted in a ditch behind a hedge, from whence they poured into our ranks a murderous fire. Finding that the enemy's front extended beyond either flank, I formed the 46th on the right of the 76th and advanced a line of skirmishers along my whole front. In this position with Lieut. Moore's section of Artillery in rear of the 76th Illinois Infantry, the Brigade kept the enemy fully engaged over two hours, until the train had safely passed.

The 8th Illinois Infantry, posted a short distance on the left of this Brigade received orders and had moved out to follow the train before I had received a similar order, which enabled the enemy to throw a large force on our left. The 76th moved off by the left flank under shelter of a rail fence which at the same time concealed the enemy. With great presence of mind, Lieut. Col. C. C. Jones of the 76th Illinois Infantry ordered his men to fire on them as soon as their position was discovered, and drove them back in confusion. The 46th changed its front and charged across the field under a heavy fire of artillery and musketry to the shelter of the woods, and then marched out upon the road to the next hill, where they were again vigorously shelled by the enemy. The 76th after repulsing the enemy moved directly to the road exposed to heavy fire, and soon after joined the Brigade.

The column moved forward with but little further opposition, until within about two miles of Clinton, where the enemy charged our rear and were repulsed with great loss, by the 11th Illinois Infantry, commanded by Capt. Vore and Lieut. More's section of Artillery. The 46th was ordered to support the 11th, but reached the ground only in time to fire a volley after the retreating foe. The 46th Illinois then relieved the 11th as rear guard, which position it held alternately with the 76th and 8th Illinois Infantry during the day. The enemy were seen several times during the day drawn up in line, but they evidently thought "discretion the better part of valor," and wisely kept out of range.

We arrived in camp at Vicksburg on the 9th without further annoyance.

It is with pride and pleasure that I refer to the conduct of the officers and soldiers of my command, many of whom were for the first time under fire. Not one left the ranks or flinched from duty during the engagement, unless compelled to do so from wounds or exhaustion. It is enough to say of them that every man did his whole duty. The field and line officers were all at their posts and did their duty so well that a few cannot be mentioned without doing manifest injury to the others.

To Lieut. Col. Sheetz and his noble regiment, the 8th Illinois Infantry, I am under great obligations for relieving my regiments as rear guards, after they had become so completely exhausted from long continued fighting and marching as to be almost unable to proceed further. Lieuts. Moore and Nichols of Bolton's Battery, are deserving of much credit for the able manner in which they handled their respective sections while with this Brigade.

Of my personal staff, Lieuts. Woodbury, Arnold, Hughes and Seizicks, I cannot speak in too high terms of praise.

Prompt in the discharge of every duty, fearless of danger, they communicated every order with such coolness and precision that they could not fail to be understood.

The list of casualties in this Brigade has been forwarded.

Very Respectfully your Obe't Servt,

B. DORNBLASER,
Colonel Commanding Brigade,.

The casualties in the regiment were as follows, viz : Killed, three ; wounded, thirty-six ; captured, one ; missing, three ; total loss, forty-five. Our wounded received but little care until our arrival at Big Black. Here their wounds were carefully dressed and every attention possible given to them. During the night of the 8th of July the sick and wounded were removed to the hospital at Vicksburg, and on the 9th the troops marched to their camps in the city. .

The wounded of the command that fell into the hands of the enemy were very kindly treated, so much so that it was spoken of in the highest terms of praise by the wounded men, and as soon as they were able an amicable exchange of prisoners was appointed. The ceremoney of exchange took place just outside the old fortifications of the city and was the ocaasion of much good feeling among the prisoners.

July 21st Maj. Gen Blair's General Order No. 5 was received, organizing the 1st Division, 17th Army Corps, the 2d Brigade of which was composed of the 11th, 46th and 76th regiments of Illinois Infantry, and Col. Dornblaser of the 46th placed in command.

July 29th the 46th, together with the 76th Illinois Infantry, embarked on board the Steamer "Adams" and proceeded down the Mississippi river to Morganza Bend, La. The Division encamped on the river bank and constructed shades and arbors for shelter from the burning sun. Drill and picket was the order, the latter of which was a very necessary as well as a rather delicate duty at times, from the fact that the enemy made frequent raids upon our picket lines from their camps on the Atchafalaya.

On the night of the 8th of August, Lieut. Col. Jones and two hundred men of the 46th went out on a scout and captured twelve gay and festive rebels who, not dreaming of danger, fell asleep and into the hands of the blue coats, and were brought into camp on the 9th.

On the 13th of August, General Canby's order No. 93 was promulgated, assigning the regiment to the 1st Brigade, 2d Division, 19th Army Corps. The Brigade to consist of the 8th, 11th, 46th and 76th regiments of Illinois infantry, and the 7th and 30th Missouri Infantry, and to be commanded by Col. B. Dornblaser of the 46th Illinois Infantry, General Dennis to command the Division, and General Reynolds the Corps.

Lieut. I. A. Arnold and Lieut. H. H. Woodbury were placed on the Brigade staff, the former as A. A. Q. M. and the latter A. A. A. Gen.

The Division was ordered to embark on transports on the 23d of August and proceed to Port Hudson, La,, where it arrived on the morning of the 24th. See report.

HEADQUARTERS 1ST BRIG. 2D DIV., 19TH A. C.
MORGANZA, LA., August 29th, 1864.

CAPTAIN W. E. KUHN,
A. A. A. Gen. 2d Div., 19th Army Corps.

Captain :—I have the honor to report that in compliance with orders, this Brigade embarked on Steamers on the night of the 23d inst., and proceeded to Port Hudson, La., where it disembarked. On the evening of the 24th instant, at five o'clock p. m., the column moved out in the direction of Clinton, La., the 1st Brigade in advance, supplied with five days rations and one ammunition wagon to each regiment. The command marched all night, only resting at intervals to enable the column to close up, and arrived at Clinton at noon of the 25th. Small scouting parties of the enemy only were encountered, who fled at our approach.

The troops rested until four o'clock p. m. of the 26th, when the return march was commenced, arriving at Port Hudson on the morning of the 28th and Morganza on the morning of the 29th.

Port Hudson is distant twenty-five miles from here, and from Port Hudson to Clinton the same. The march was a very hard one and the losses sustained by the Brigade were caused principally by men becoming exhausted by the way and being captured by the enemy, who followed in our rear. The following are the losses of the Brigade : 11th Illinois, three missing; 46th Illinois, two missing; 76th Illinois, one missing; 30th Missouri, two missing.

Respectfully your Obed't Serv't.
B. BORNBLASER,
Colonel Commanding Brigade.

Orders were received September 2d to embark early on the morning of the 3d, with all the camp and garrison equippage of the command. Left Morganza at four a. m. on the 4th; proceeded up the river and arrived at the mouth of White River, Ark., without incident of note, on the 8th of September, and went into camp on a large cotton plantation. The ground was speedily cleared of the luxuriant cotton plant and the camp fitted up in splendid style.

On the 13th of September Chaplain Lewis started with the

non-veterans of A, B and C, whose term of service had expired. They were to proceed to Springfield, Illinois, to be mustered out of service.

The only incident worthy of note occurring during the stay of the regiment at the Mouth of White River, was a tremendous storm of wind and rain on the night of the 28th, which leveled every tent and flooded the camp with water. The sudden waking up of over two thousand men to find their frail shelters swept away and themselves drenched to the skin by the pouring rain, caused a conglomeration of the most hideous and ludricious sounds ever heard or made by man. While some were making frantic yet vain efforts to hold up their tents against the storm, others—and many officers of both high and low degree—could be seen by the vivid lightning's glare, "scudding under bare poles" from one demolished shelter to another, doomed to a similar fate. A company of men in one portion of the camp would hurrah for McClellan which would be answered from another portion by the shout of a whole regiment for Lincoln. A cheer for Valandigham or Jeff Davis would be answered by a whole Brigade with curses and groans. Slang phrases, such as "here's your mule," &c., &c., were the common utterances of those in busy search of lost clothing, tents and baggage. The incidents of the night furnished a rich theme for ludicrous comment and laughter, which served to while away many tedious hours in camp.

A short distance from camp were numerous ponds or lakes containing large quantities of fine fish, the catching of which furnished much sport. The modus operandi of catching them was novel. Twenty or thirty soldiers would divest themselves of their clothing, arm themselves with clubs of about four feet in length, form a skirmish line across one end of the lake and advance, beating the water and thus drive the fish before them into the shallow water at the other end of the lake, then woe to the unlucky fish that would show his head, his fate would be sure to be sealed by a blow from a club. In the excitement of the chase many a blow aimed at the head of a fish would descend on the head or back of some unlucky biped of an entirely different species. Such accidents would call forth peals of laughter and the injured party would pass it off in the most philosophical good humor.

On the 6th of October the 1st Brigade, 3d Division, 19th Army Corps, and the 46th Illinois Infantry, all under the command of Lieut. Col. Jones of the 46th, were ordered to embark, to proceed to Duvall's Bluff, Arkansas. They left the mouth of White River at sunrise, October 7th, and arrived at Duvall's Bluff on the 9th. The regiment went into camp south of the Landing and commenced building log barracks which they soon completed. The regiment was highly complimented by General C. C. Andrews commanding Post, for its skill and energy in building such neat and comfortable barracks in so short a time. At this place the regiment also did much fatigue duty on the fortifications, which were extensive and incomplete. The wet weather and peculiar character of the soil made their duty very arduous. As an offset for this, however, the large number of deer on the prairies near by afforded profitable amusement for the sportsmen of the command, who brought in five or six fine deer every day they went out, and one day fourteen were killed and brought into the regiment.

The fine barracks built by the regiment had to be given up, as orders were received on the 27th of November to embark on transports for Memphis, Tenn. Left Duvall's Bluff at one o'clock p. m., of the 28th, and arrived at the mouth of White River at three o'clock, p. m. of the 29th, and Memphis on the 1st of December at six o'clock, p. m.

While coming down White River, Arkansas, on the 28th a party of guerillas fired on the boat and wounded three men, none severely. The fire was quickly returned by the regiment. On the same night Thomas Walbridge, a Private of company "K," fell overboard and was drowned. His body could not be recovered.

At Memphis the regiment went into camp on the Pigeon Roost road, just east of the city. While at this camp all the non-veteran soldiers of H, E. I. K and F, were mustered out of the service, together with Major McCracken, Captain Hughes, Stewart, Wakefield, Reitzell, and Lieutenants Terry, Shaw and McKibben.

The command suffered here from cold by reason of shelter, tents and scarcity of timber and fuel. The tents were no protection against cold, and the want of timber or lumber prevented the men from building comfortable huts or barracks.

On the 12th of December orders from General Canby were received re-organizing the troops of the 19th army corps into the Reserve Corps, Military Division of West Mississippi. The 2d Brigade, which was composed of the 8th, 11th, 46th and 76th regiments of Illinois Infantry, and the 23d Wisconsin and 30th Missouri regiments Infantry, was commanded by Brig. Gen. E. S. Dennis.

Early on the morning of the 21st of December an expedition started out, commanded by Brig. Gen. Lawler, going in the direction of La Grange, Tenn. The 8th, 11th and 46th Illinois Infantry, commanded by Colonel Dornblaser of the 46th, was accompanied by two other small brigades and marched the first day to Germantown, second to Moscow, and third to Wolf River near Moscow, Tenn., where we remained until early on the morning of the 26th of December, when the return march to Memphis was commenced. Col. Kent's Brigade marched to Collierville and encamped. Col. Dornblaser's Brigade encamped three miles west of Colliersville on the Bailey plantation, and Col. Green's Brigade at Germantown and White's Station. This disposition of troops was made with a view to guard the railroad, which had been repaired from Memphis to Colliersville, against the numerous bands of guerilla parties prowling through this section of the country.

On the 31st of December the troops were all brought to Memphis by rail and ordered to be ready to embark without delay.

The 46th, with the exception of four companies that were put aboard the "Autocrat," embarked on the Steamer "Marble City," on the morning of the 2d of January, 1865, and proceeded to Kennerville, La., twenty-five miles from New Orleans by water, and disembarked. The camp at this place was protected from overflow by the levee, but the rainy season made it exceedingly muddy. It was a complete "stick-in-the-mud" camp.

The regiment marched to Lakeport on Lake Pontchartrain on the 4th of February, and embarked on the Steamers "Planter" and "Alabama" on the 7th and 8th of February, and proceeded to Fort Gaines, Dauphin Island, Ala., at which place we arrived and went into camp on the 9th and 10th of February. While the camp at Kennerville, La., was pure mud, at this place it was pure white sand. However, the discomforts of the camp were fully neutralized by the pleasure and profit afforded catching and eating oysters, which wers found in great abundance in the bay close by.

Col. Dornblaser having been home on a leave of absence, returned to the regiment on the first of March, bringing with him one hundred and sixty recruits, filling up the regiment to nine hundred and twenty-two men, aggregate strength. This made the 46th one of the largest regiments in the command.

While here the Reserve Corps was re-organized and called the 13th army corps, to be commanded by Major General Gordon Granger. The 8th, 11th and 46th Illinois Infantry, comprised the 2d Brigade of the 1st Division, and Gen. E. S. Dennis assigned to the command of the same. Brig. Gen. James C. Veatch commanded the Division.

On the 17th of March all the surplus baggage, camp and garrison equippage was turned in to the Post Quartermaster and the troops fitted for an active land campaign. The Brigade was transferred to the opposite side of Mobile Bay the same evening, and commenced its march on Mobile early on the morning of the 18th. On the 20th we reached Oyster Bay where Gen. Benton's Division of the 13th Army Corps were constructing corduroy causeways through the swamps. Our Division was detailed until the morning of the 22d of March to enable Benton's Division to get ahead. On the night of the 20th a tremendous rainstorm caused the temporary bridges built to be washed away, making it necessary to reconstruct them. The work was arduous and disagreeable, but was accomplished without unnecessary grumbling. In consequence of the great difficulty of getting the train through the deep sand and mud and over the rough corduroys, the column did not reach the vicinity of Spanish Fort, the first rebel stronghold on our line of march—until the evening of the 21st of March. Early on the morning of the 22d the Fort was invested, much to the surprise of the rebels, as they did not deem it possible for us to advance so rapidly over the obstacles we had to encounter.

After the Fort was invested, the 46th was ordered to guard the approaches from the rear, as it was reported that the enemy had a large force of cavalry in that direction threatening an attack.

On the 31st of March the 1st Division, 13th Army Corps, took charge of a supply train to Gen. Steele's command near Blakely, Ala. The 46th was left in charge of the baggage train of the Division until the 4th of April, when it moved with the train and joined the Division near Sibley's Mills, east of Blakely.

During the siege of Blakely the 1st Division, 13th Army Corps occupied a front line of about three-fourths of a mile in extent between Andrews Division of the 13th Army Corps and Garrard's Division of the 16th Army Corps, which required but from two to three regiments to fill the space, consequently the troops in front would be daily relieved by others. On the evening of the 5th of April, the 46th Illinois Infantry was ordered to relieve the 8th Illinois Infantry in the trenches, and advance the line during the night and construct a new line of works. Companies G and B were deployed as skirmishers and sent forward early in the evening to establish a line twenty-five yards in advance on the right, and one hundred on the left. The position was gained with but little opposition and the work of throwing up earthworks vigorously commenced. The rebel sharpshooters constantly kept stimulating our working parties to renewed efforts by sending minnie balls whistling over every portion of the line at intervals uncomfortably short. At about two o'clock a. m. of the 6th of April, the enemy made a vigorous attack upon our lines with a view to dislodge our working parties, but were handsomely repulsed. In this action Private Andrew Hess of company "B" was mortally wounded by a fragment of a shell. This was our only casualty, owing to the completeness of our defenses.

On the 8th of April, Spanish Fort was captured, and on the evening of the 9th Fort Blakely was charged and taken also. In this action the 8th Illinois as skirmishers, followed by the 11th and 46th Illinois as supports were amont the first to reach the Fort, but were prevented from following up and capturing their share of prisoners by reason of an order to withdraw to the outside of the works as soon as they had entered and formed inside of the same, thus enabling Garrard's Division to sweep down to the Bay in front of our Brigade and capture the prisoners. After securing these, and the arms, cannon and trophies, the Brigade marched to its camp.

April 10th the Division marched four miles in the direction of the Alabama River and made preparations for a march into the interior, but on the 11th of April news of the probable evacuation of Mobile was received, in consequence of which the troops were marched back to Stark's Landing during the night, and embarked at daylight on the morning of the 12th of April. At nine o'clock a. m., the fleet sailed from the landing in the direction of Mobile, and at eleven o'clock a, m. arrived at the Shell Road Landing, five miles below the city. The city authorities surrendered the place and its defenses to the Army and Navy of the United States on the 12th of April, and the city was occupied by the troops on the same day.

The regiment went into camp in the western limits of the city, where a comfortable camp was soon fitted up.

On the 16th of April the glorious tidings of Lee's surrender to General Grant was confirmed and greeted with shouts of joy as the forerunner of the speedy overthrow of the entire rebellion. But the echoing sounds of exultation had not yet died away, when on the 20th the horrible news of the assassination of President Lincoln burst upon us like a clap of thunder from a clear sky, causing our rejoicing to be turned to bitter grief.

April 21st the 11th and 46th regiments Illinois Infantry marched to Whistler seven miles out and returned, in consequence of a report that a rebel force was threatening the place, which proved untrue.

The time of the Regiment was principally taken up with drill and inspections while in this camp, and never did it present a more formidable and soldierly appearance since its first appearance, and as such received many compliments.

On the eighth of May, Gen. Dick Taylor surrendered his army to Gen. Canby, who at once sent commissioners to Meridian, Columbus, Jackson and other prominent points to parole the men and receive the public property.

Major Chase, Paymaster U. S. A., paid the Regiment on the 11th and 12th of May, up to February 28, 1865. On the morning of the 13th the Regiment left Mobile on the cars for Meridian, Miss., where it arrived on the 14th. Part of the Regiment was at once sent to Columbus, Macon, Gainesville, Gainesville Junction and Lauderdale Springs, Miss., to take charge of public property. The Regiment was relieved by troops from the 16th A. C. and Gen. Grierson's command, and ordered to Mobile, where it arrived in detachments from the 18th until the 21st of May, and occupied its old camp. Col. Dornblaser of the 46th was again assigned to the command of the 2d Brigade on the 24th of May, and on the 27th the 1st and 2d Brigades of the Division embarked on steamers for New Orleans. The 46th went aboard the "J. H. Groesbeck," and arrived without accident to Hickox Landing at the Lake end and of the New Orleans Shell Road on the 28th of May, and at once disembarked and marched to the race track near the "Halfway House," where it went into camp. On the 30th of May the troops embarked at

New Orleans to proceed to Alexandria, Natchitoches and Shreveport on Red River, to receive the surrender of Kirby Smith's Trans-Mississippi rebel army. Landed at Shreveport, La., on the 8th of June, after one of the most tedious and disagreeable voyages imaginable. The crowded condition of the boats and extreme heat of the weather, caused much discomfort and sickness.

June 19th the Regiment embarked on steamer Peerless and proceeded to Grand Ecore, La., to relieve the 21st Iowa Infantry on duty at Natchitoches, Salubrity Springs and Grand Ecore. Gen. Taylor's army was encamped at Salubrity Springs, prior to his march to the Rio Grande in 1846. The Regiment performed garrison duty here until November 20th, when it marched via Pleasant Hill and Mansfield, La., to Shreveport. Major Clingman with companies E and G of the 46th Illinois, and Co. A of the 19th Pa. Cavalry went to Marshall, Texas, to relieve the 8th Illinois Infantry on duty there.

The garrison of Shreveport consisted of eight companies of the 46th Illinois, the 80th U. S. Colored Infantry and company C, 19th Pa. Cavalry. On the 27th of December, Gen. Canby's special order No. 140 was received ordering the Regiment to proceed to Baton Rouge, La., and Springfield, Illinois, for muster out and final discharge. The low stage of water in Red River made it impossible for the whole Regiment to embark on one boat, hence it left Shreveport on various steamers from the 1st to the 4th of January, 1866, and arrived at Baton Rouge on the 10th of January. As soon as the Regiment was comfortably situated in camp the whole available clerical force of the same was put to work making up muster out rolls. On the 20th of January the Regiment was mustered out and at once embarked on steamer Lady Gay for Cairo, arriving at that place on the 25th, thence proceeded by Railroad to Camp Butler, Illinois, where it arrived on the evening of the 27th. Through the usual energy of the officers of the Regiment, and the extreme kindness and courtesy of Major Cleghorn, A. A. G., Col. Bridgman and Major Grover, Paymasters, the Regiment received its final pay and discharge on the 1st of February, after a stay in camp of only five days. An extra train was in readiness to convey the men to Decatur, Illinois. in time for the train North on the Central Road, of which they eagerly took advantage in order to reach their several homes with the least delay.

Thus closes the Record of the 46th Illinois Veteran Volunteer Infantry. Its organization has been kept up nearly four and a half years. Over seventeen hundred men have been members of it, and its line of march and travel has extended over ten thousand miles.

While with thankful hearts we acknowledge the preservation of our health and lives to enable us to return to and enjoy our homes and friends, let us ever hold in kind remembrance those of our companions who lost their lives in the great contest, and whose graves can be found from the Ohio to the Gulf.

As our record as a Regiment has been bright and honorable, let each and all resolve to perpetuate that record by individual virtue and honesty as citizens, that none may descend to the grave "unhonored and unsung."

To our friends at home, whose loving eyes were ever following us, whose prayers constantly ascended to the throne of God for our welfare, and who stood ready with outstretched arms to welcome us to our homes, let us ever be grateful.

www.ingramcontent.com/pod-product-compliance
Lightning Source LLC
Chambersburg PA
CBHW022144090426
42742CB00010B/1387